REDEMPTION
Accomplished and Applied

REDEMPTION

Accomplished and Applied

John Murray

William B. Eerdmans Publishing Company
Grand Rapids, Michigan

Wm. B. Eerdmans Publishing Co.
2140 Oak Industrial Drive NE, Grand Rapids, Michigan 49505
www.eerdmans.com

27 26 25 24   20 19 18

Library of Congress Cataloging-in-Publication Data

Murray, John, 1898-1975.
Redemption accomplished and applied / John Murray.
pages   cm
Originally published: 1955.
Includes bibliographical references and indexes.
ISBN 978-0-8028-7309-5 (pbk.: alk. paper)
1. Redemption.   I. Title.

BT775.M8   2015
234'.3 — dc23
                                    2015009844

Scriptures taken from the King James Version

Contents

CONTENTS

Foreword to the 2015 Edition

A s a new convert to Christianity in the mid-1980s, I was always trying to find books that would help me engage more deeply with the faith. Because I had not grown up in a Christian home and had almost never attended church, my knowledge of the Bible and of its teaching was minimal. I knew something about God, something about sin, and something about Christ. Beyond that, I was a Cambridge undergraduate with less theological understanding than a ten-year-old who had been taught the catechism.

Because of this, I was always hunting for good, basic books on Christian doctrine. A kind local pastor gave me a copy of J. I. Packer's *God's Words* and that helped introduce me to the basic elements of evangelical theology. Then someone recommended I obtain a copy of John Murray, *Redemption Accomplished and Applied*. I had never heard of Murray and neither had the manager of the local Christian bookshop, but he dutifully ordered me a copy. When it arrived, I confess to a little disappointment. Frankly, I had expected a weightier tome, not a relatively brief paperback. Yet my disappointment did not survive even my reading of the very first chapter.

What Murray did, and what I had never really seen before, was demonstrate how my salvation connected to the work of God in both eternity, as he planned salvation, and time, as he executed it in the person and work of his Son and applied it to individuals through the work of his Holy Spirit. Thus, Murray's little book did three things of major importance: it showed how eternity and time relate to each other in salvation, how that salvation is a Trinitarian matter, rooted in the very identity of God as Trinity, and how this makes sense of the whole Bible.

Of course, Murray was not really doing anything exceptional. What he did was build upon a rich tradition of thinking in the Reformed churches, which placed each of these three points in the foundation of their testimony. As a minister in my own denomination, the Orthodox Presbyterian Church, and as a key faculty member in the early days of Westminster Theological Seminary, Murray loved the Westminster Standards and the theology which they teach. What he sought to do was to explicate that theology, particularly as it relates to salvation.

More specifically, Murray was seeking to articulate the *order of salvation* (Latin: *ordo salutis*) in a manner that also connected it to the *history of salvation* (Latin: *historia salutis*). We might distinguish the two by saying that the order of salvation pertains to the way in which the individual appropriates salvation. Election, calling, justification, sanctification, and glorification are the basic elements of this. The history of salvation is focused on the acts of God in history, specifically as they culminate in the work of the Lord Jesus Christ, which provide the basis for the order of salvation.

Thus the work begins with a careful analysis of the nature of the atonement. This is history of salvation territory. Christ's incarnation and death must be understood against the backdrop of God's love in eternity for those he has chosen to rescue from their sin and its eternal consequences. Then the cross itself must be understood in terms of God's wrath against sin, of his imputation of our sin to Christ, and of the Old Testament sacrificial system of which it is the ful-fillment. Murray's view is profoundly particularist, whereby Christ's death is not for everyone but for those whom God has chosen.

Then, in the second half of the work, Murray looks at the implications of Christ's death for the salvation of the individ-ual believer, addressing the various elements of the order of salvation. What emerges is a seamless move from eternity to time, and from the work of God in Christ to the work of God in the believer.

Murray's book has its critics. His view of particular re-demption is repudiated by those opposed to what they call "limited atonement," who see it as restricting God's love and standing at odds with passages in the New Testament which apparently speak of the universality of God's desire for all to be saved. Others within the Reformed camp itself have taken issue with Murray, or at least with certain traditions of reading Murray, for what they see as a failure to distinguish clearly between justification and sanctification.

I make no comment on those debates here. The book you have in your hand is a miniature masterpiece of theology, dealing reverently on every page with matters of great theo-logical significance. Whether you end the book by agreeing or disagreeing with its author, you will have found your own thinking on these issues sharpened and clarified.

CARL R. TRUEMAN
Paul Woolley Professor of Church History
Westminster Theological Seminary, Philadelphia, PA
Pastor, Cornerstone Presbyterian Church (OPC), Ambler, PA

Preface to the First Edition

The accomplishment of redemption or, as it has frequently been called, the atonement, is central in our Christian faith. It is no wonder therefore that the Christian church should have in its possession a rich repertory of literature on this subject. It is with some misgiving that I have ventured to offer for publication the following attempt to deal with an aspect of the divine revelation that has been explored to such an extent. This present study cannot pretend to be in the same class as many of the superb contributions of both the more remote and the more recent past. I can only claim that I am presenting what has passed through the crucible of my own reflection. I am conscious of the profound debt I owe to numberless theologians and expositors. Acknowledgment in details would be impossible. Other men have labored and we have entered into their labors. However, there are certain facets of this great truth which I have sought to bring into clearer focus. Perhaps some neglected factors have received an emphasis which our present-day theological situation demands.

On so great a theme as Christ's redemptive accomplishment I am profoundly conscious of the limitations that encompass our attempts at exposition. Thought and expression stagger in the presence of the spectacle that confronts us in the vicarious sin-bearing of the Lord of glory. Here we must realize that we are dealing with the mystery of godliness, and eternity will not reach the bottom of it nor exhaust its praise. Yet it is ours to proclaim it and continue the attempt to expound and defend its truth.

The material in Part II of this volume, dealing with the application of redemption, was written for *The Presbyterian Guardian* at the request of the editor, the Rev. Leslie W. Sloat, and was published in twenty-two articles from October 1952 to August 1954. I wish to express my indebtedness to *The Presbyterian Guardian* and to Mr. Sloat in particular for the courtesy of publication and for permission to reprint these articles in the present form. Any difference there may be in the mode of treatment between Part I and Part II of this volume is explained by the original purpose of what is comprised in the latter.

I wish to extend my gratitude to Miss Margaret S. Robinson for her services in preparing the typescript and to Miss T. E. N. Ozinga for preparing the indexes. Above all, I must thank the publishers, the Wm. B. Eerdmans Publishing Company, for undertaking this publication and for the many courtesies bestowed upon me in negotiations to that end.

I can only hope that the reader will find these studies consonant with the witness of Holy Scripture as the only infallible rule of faith and that by God's grace what is accordant with Scripture will elicit the response of faith and conviction.

Philadelphia   JOHN MURRAY
May 24, 1955

PART I

Redemption Accomplished

CHAPTER I

The Necessity of the Atonement

The accomplishment of redemption is concerned with what has been generally called the atonement. No treatment of the atonement can be properly oriented that does not trace its source to the free and sovereign love of God. It is with this perspective that the best known text in the Bible provides us: "For God so loved the world that he gave his only begotten Son, that whosoever believeth in him should not perish, but have everlasting life" (John 3:16). Here we have an ultimate of divine revelation and therefore of human thought. Beyond this we cannot and dare not go.

That it is an ultimate of human thought does not exclude, however, any further characterization of this love of God. The Scripture informs us that this love of God from which the atonement flows and of which it is the expression is a love that is distinguishing. No one gloried in this love of God more than the apostle Paul. "God commendeth his own love toward us, in that, while we were yet sinners, Christ died for us" (Rom. 5:8). "What shall we then say to these things? If God be for us, who can be against us? He that spared not his own Son but delivered him up for us all, how shall he not with him also freely give us all things?" (Rom. 8:31-32). But it is the same apostle who delineates for us the eternal counsel of God which supplies the background of such protestation and which defines

3

for us the orbit within which such statements have meaning and validity. He writes: "For whom he did foreknow, he also did predestinate to be conformed to the image of his Son, that he might be the firstborn among many brethren" (Rom. 8:29). And elsewhere he becomes perhaps even more explicit when he says: "He chose us in him before the foundation of the world, that we should be holy and without blame before him; in love having predestinated us unto the adoption of children through Jesus Christ to himself, according to the good pleasure of his will" (Eph. 1:4-5). The love of God from which the atonement springs is not a distinctionless love; it is a love that elects and predestinates. God was pleased to set his invincible and everlasting love upon a countless multitude and it is the determinate purpose of this love that the atonement secures.

It is necessary to underline this concept of sovereign love. Truly God is love. Love is not something adventitious; it is not something that God may choose to be or choose not to be. He is love, and that necessarily, inherently, and eternally. As God is spirit, as he is light, so he is love. Yet it belongs to the very essence of electing love to recognize that it is not inherently necessary to that love which God necessarily and eternally is that he should set such love as issues in redemption and adoption upon utterly undesirable and hell-deserving objects. It was of the free and sovereign good pleasure of his will, a good pleasure that emanated from the depths of his own goodness, that he chose a people to be heirs of God and joint-heirs with Christ. The reason resides wholly in himself and proceeds from determinations that are peculiarly his as the "I am that I am." The atonement does not win or constrain the love of God. The love of God constrains to the atonement as the means of accomplishing love's determinate purpose.[1]

---

1. Cf. Hugh Martin: *The Atonement: in its Relations to the Covenant, the Priesthood, the Intercession of our Lord* (Edinburgh, 1887), p. 19.

It must be regarded, therefore, as a settled datum that the love of God is the cause or source of the atonement. But this does not answer the question as to the *reason* or *necessity*. What is the *reason* why the love of God should take such a way of realizing its end and fulfilling its purpose? Why, we are compelled to ask, the sacrifice of the Son of God, why the blood of the Lord of glory? "For what necessity and for what reason," asked Anselm of Canterbury, "did God, since he is omnipotent, take upon himself the humiliation and weakness of human nature in order to its restoration."[2] Why did not God realize the purpose of his love for mankind by the word of his power and the fiat of his will? If we say that he could not, do we not impugn his power? If we say that he could but would not, do we not impugn his wisdom? Such questions are not scholastic subleties or vain curiosities. To evade them is to miss something that is central in the interpretation of the redeeming work of Christ and to miss the vision of some of its essential glory. Why did God become man? Why, having become man, did he die? Why, having died, did he die the accursed death of the cross? This is the question of the *necessity* of the atonement.

Among the answers given to this question, two are most important. They are, first, the view known as that of hypothetical necessity and, second, the view which we may call that of consequent absolute necessity. The former was held by such notable men as Augustine and Thomas Aquinas.[3] The latter may be regarded as the more classic protestant position.

The view known as that of hypothetical necessity main-

2. *Cur. Deus Homo*, Lib. I, Cap. I: "qua necessitate scilicet et ratione deus, cum sit omnipotens, humilitatem et infirmitatem humanae naturae pro eius restauratione assumpserit."
3. *Cf.* Augustine: *On the Trinity*, Bk. XIII, Chap. 10; Aquinas: *Summa Theologica*, Part III, Q. 46, Arts 2 and 3.

tains that God could have forgiven sin and saved his elect without atonement or satisfaction — other means were open to God to whom all things are possible. But the way of the vicarious sacrifice of the Son of God was the way which God in his grace and sovereign wisdom chose because this is the way in which the greatest number of advantages concur and the way in which grace is more marvellously exhibited. So, while God could save without an atonement, yet, in accordance with his sovereign decree, he actually does not. Without shedding of blood there is actually no remission or salvation. Yet nothing inheres in the nature of God or in the nature of remission of sin that makes blood-shedding indispensable.

The other view we call consequent absolute necessity. The word "consequent" in this designation points to the fact that God's will or decree to save any is of free and sovereign grace. To save lost men was not of absolute necessity but of the sovereign good pleasure of God. The terms "absolute necessity," however, indicate that God, having elected some to everlasting life out of his mere good pleasure, was under the necessity of accomplishing this purpose through the sacrifice of his own Son, a necessity arising from the perfections of his own nature. In a word, while it was not inherently necessary for God to save, yet, since salvation had been purposed, it was necessary to secure this salvation through a satisfaction that could be rendered only through substitutionary sacrifice and blood-bought redemption.[4]

It might appear to be vainly speculative and presumptuous to press such an inquiry and to try to determine what is inherently necessary for God. Furthermore, it might appear

4. Cf. Francis Turretin: Institutio Theologiae Elencticae, Loc. XIV, Q. X; James Henley Thornwell: "The Necessity of the Atonement" in Collected Writings, Vol. II (Richmond, 1886), pp. 205-261; George Stevenson: A Dissertation on the Atonement (Philadelphia, 1832), pp. 5-98; A. A. Hodge: The Atonement (London, 1868), pp. 217-222.

to lie on the face of such a text as, "without the shedding of blood there is no remission" that the extent of revelation to us is simply that there is *de facto* no remission without blood-shedding and that it would be beyond the warrant of Scripture for us to say what is *de jure* indispensable for God.

But it is not presumptuous for us to say that certain things are inherently necessary or impossible for God. It belongs to our faith in God to avow that he cannot lie and that he cannot deny himself. Such divine "cannots" are his glory and for us to refrain from reckoning with such "impossibles" would be to deny God's glory and perfection.

The question really is: does the Scripture provide us with evidence or considerations on the basis of which we may conclude that this is one of the things impossible or necessary for God, impossible for him to save sinners without vicarious sacrifice and inherently necessary, therefore, that salvation freely and sovereignly determined, should be accomplished by the blood-shedding of the Lord of glory. The following Scriptural considerations appear to require an affirmative answer. In adducing these considerations it must be remembered that they are to be viewed in co-ordination and in their cumulative effect.

1. There are those passages which create a very strong presumption in favor of this inference. In Hebrews 2:10, 17, for example, it is estimated that it was divinely appropriate that the Father in bringing many sons unto glory should make the captain of their salvation perfect through sufferings and that it behooved the Savior himself to be made in all things like unto his brethren. The force of such expressions is scarcely satisfied by the notion that it was merely consonant with the wisdom and love of God to accomplish salvation in this way. This is true, of course, and is maintained on the view known as that of hypothetical necessity. But more appears to be said in this passage. The case appears to be rather that

7

such were the exigencies of the purpose of grace that the dictates of divine propriety required that salvation should be accomplished through a captain of salvation who would be made perfect through sufferings and that this entailed for the captain of salvation that he be made in all things like unto his brethren. In other words, we are carried beyond the thought of consonance with the divine character to the thought of divine properties which made it requisite that the many sons should be brought to glory in this particular way. If this is the case, then we are led to the thought that exigencies of divine import are met by the sufferings of the captain of salvation.

2. There are passages, such as John 3:14-16, which rather definitely suggest that the alternative to the giving of God's only-begotten Son and his being lifted up on the accursed tree is the eternal perdition of the lost. The eternal peril to which the lost are exposed is remedied by the giving of the Son. But we can hardly escape the additional thought that there is no other alternative.

3. Such passages as Hebrews 1:1-3; 2:9-18; 9:9-14, 22-28 teach very plainly that the efficacy of Christ's work is contingent upon the unique constitution of Christ's person. This fact does not of itself establish the point in question. But contextual considerations reveal further implications. The emphasis in these passages rests upon the finality, perfection, and transcendent efficacy of Christ's sacrifice. Such finality, perfection, and efficacy are necessitated by the gravity of sin, and sin must be effectively removed if salvation is to be realized. It is this consideration that gives such strength to the necessity, spoken of in 9:23, to the effect that while the patterns of things in the heavenlies should be purified with the blood of goats and calves, the heavenly things themselves should be purified by the blood of none other than the Son. In other words, there is stated to be a necessity that can be met by nothing less than the blood of Jesus. But the blood of

Jesus is blood that has the requisite efficacy and virtue only by reason of the fact that he who is the Son, the effulgence of the Father's glory and the express image of his substance, became himself also partaker of flesh and blood and thus was able by one sacrifice to perfect all those who are sanctified. It is surely not an unwarranted inference to conclude that the thought here presented is that only such a person, offering such a sacrifice, could have dealt with sin so as to remove it and could have made such purification as would secure for the many sons to be brought to glory access into the very holiest of the divine presence. And this is but saying that the blood-shedding of Jesus was necessary to the ends contemplated and secured.

There are other considerations, also, which may be derived from these passages, especially Hebrews 9:9-14, 22-28. They are the considerations which arise from the fact that Christ's own sacrifice is the great exemplar after which the Levitical sacrifices were patterned. We often think of the Levitical sacrifices as providing the pattern for the sacrifice of Christ. This direction of thought is not improper — the Levitical sacrifices do furnish us with the categories in terms of which we are to interpret the sacrifice of Christ, particularly the categories of expiation, propitiation, and reconciliation. But this line of thought is not the characteristic one in Hebrews 9. The thought is specifically that the Levitical sacrifices were patterned after the heavenly exemplar — they were "patterns of the things in the heavens" (Heb. 9:23). Hence the necessity for the blood offerings of the Levitical economy arose from the fact that the exemplar after which they were fashioned was a blood offering, the transcendent blood offering by which the heavenly things were purified. The necessity of blood-shedding in the Levitical ordinance is simply a necessity arising from the necessity of blood-shedding in the higher realm of the heavenly. Now our question is: what kind of necessity is this that obtained in the realm of the heavenly? Was it merely hypothetical or was it absolute? The following observations will indicate the answer.

(a) The emphasis of the context is that the transcendent efficacy of Christ's sacrifice is required by the exigencies arising from sin. And these exigencies are not hypothetical — they are absolute. The logic of this emphasis upon the intrinsic gravity of sin and the necessity of its removal does not comport with the idea of hypothetical necessity — the reality and gravity of sin make effective expiation indispensable, and that is to say absolutely necessary.

(b) The precise nature of Christ's priestly offering and the efficacy of his sacrifice are bound up with the constitution of his person. If there was the necessity for such a sacrifice in order to remove sin, none other but he could offer such a sacrifice. And this amounts to the necessity of such a person offering such a sacrifice.

(c) In this passage the heavenly things in connection with which Christ's blood was shed are called *true*. The contrast implied is not true as opposed to false or real as opposed to fictitious. It is the heavenly as contrasted with the earthly, the eternal with the temporary, the complete with the partial, the final with the provisional, the abiding with that which passes away. When we think of the sacrifice of Christ as offered in connection with things answering to that characterization — heavenly, eternal, complete, final, abiding, is it not impossible to think of this sacrifice as only hypothetically necessary in the accomplishment of God's design of bringing many sons to glory? If the sacrifice of Christ is only hypothetically necessary, then the heavenly things in connection with which it had relevance and meaning were also only hypothetically necessary. And that is surely a difficult hypothesis.

The sum of the matter is that a necessity (Heb. 9:23) for the blood-shedding of Christ unto the remission of sins (vers. 14, 22, 26) is here propounded and it is a necessity without reservation or qualification.

4. The salvation which the election of grace involves on either view of the necessity of the atonement is salvation from sin unto holiness and fellowship with God. But if we are to think of salvation thus conceived in terms that are compatible with the holiness and righteousness of God, this salvation must embrace not merely the forgiveness of sin but also justification. And it must be a justification that takes account of our situation as condemned and guilty. Such a justification implies the necessity of a righteousness that will be adequate to our situation. Grace indeed reigns but a grace reigning apart from righteousness is not only not actual; it is inconceivable. Now, what righteousness is equal to the justification of sinners? The only righteousness conceivable that will meet the requirements of our situation as sinners and meet the requirements of a full and irrevocable justification is the righteousness of Christ. This implies his obedience and therefore his incarnation, death, and resurrection. In a word, the necessity of the atonement is inherent in and essential to justification. A salvation from sin divorced from justification is an impossibility and justification of sinners without the God-righteousness of the Redeemer is unthinkable. We can hardly escape the relevance of Paul's word: "For if a law had been given which could make alive, verily righteousness would have been by the law" (Gal. 3:21). What Paul is insisting upon is that if justification could have been secured by any other method than that of faith in Christ, by that method it would have been.

5. The cross of Christ is the supreme demonstration of the love of God (Rom. 5:8; 1 John 4:10). The supreme character of the demonstration resides in the extreme costliness of the sacrifice rendered. It is this costliness that Paul has in view when he writes: "He that spared not his own Son, but deliv-

ered him up for us all, how shall he not with him also freely give us all things?" (Rom. 8:32). The costliness of the sacrifice assures us of the greatness of the love and guarantees the bestowal of all other free gifts.

We must ask, however: would the cross of Christ be a supreme exhibition of love if there were no necessity for such costliness? Is it not so that the only inference on the basis of which the cross of Christ can be commended to us as the supreme exhibition of divine love is that the exigencies provided for required nothing less than the sacrifice of the Son of God? On that assumption we can understand John's utterance, "Herein is love, not that we loved God, but that he loved us and sent his Son to be a propitiation for our sins" (1 John 4:10). Without it we are bereft of the elements necessary to make intelligible to us the meaning of Calvary and the marvel of its supreme love to us men.

6. Finally, there is the argument from the vindicatory justice of God. Sin is the contradiction of God and he must react against it with holy indignation. This is to say that sin must meet with divine judgment (cf. Deut. 27:26; Nah. 1:2; Hab. 1:13; Rom. 1:17; 3:21-26; Gal. 3:10, 13). It is this inviolable sanctity of God's law, the immutable dictate of holiness and the unflinching demand of justice, that makes mandatory the conclusion that salvation from sin without expiation and propitiation is inconceivable. It is this principle that explains the sacrifice of the Lord of glory, the agony of Gethsemane, and the abandonment of the accursed tree. It is this principle that undergirds the great truth that God is just and the justifier of him that believeth in Jesus. For in the work of Christ the dictates of holiness and the demands of justice have been fully vindicated. God set him forth to be a propitiation to declare his righteousness.

For these reasons we are constrained to conclude that the kind of necessity which the Scriptural considerations support is that which may be described as absolute or indispensable. The proponents of hypothetical necessity do not reckon sufficiently with the exigencies involved in salvation from sin unto eternal life; they do not take proper account of the Godward aspects of Christ's accomplishment. If we keep in view the gravity of sin and the exigencies arising from the holiness of God which must be met in salvation from it, then the doctrine of indispensable necessity makes Calvary intelligible to us and enhances the incomprehensible marvel of both Calvary itself and the sovereign purpose of love which Calvary fulfilled. The more we emphasize the inflexible demands of justice and holiness the more marvelous become the love of God and its provisions.

CHAPTER II

The Nature of the Atonement

In dealing with the nature of the atonement it is well to try to discover some comprehensive category under which the various aspects of Biblical teaching may be subsumed. The more specific categories in terms of which the Scripture sets forth the atoning work of Christ are sacrifice, propitiation, reconciliation, and redemption. But we may properly ask if there is not some more inclusive rubric under which these more specific categories may be comprehended.

The Scripture regards the work of Christ as one of obedience and uses this term, or the concept that it designates, with sufficient frequency to warrant the conclusion that obedience is generic and therefore embracive enough to be viewed as the unifying or integrating principle. We should readily appreciate the propriety of this conclusion when we remember that the one passage in the Old Testament that above all others delineates the pattern of Christ's atonement is Isaiah 53. But we ask: in what capacity is the suffering personage of Isaiah 53 viewed? It is none other than that of servant. It is by that designation he is introduced, "Behold my servant shall deal prudently" (Isa. 52:13). And it is in that capacity that he reaps the justifying fruit, "By his knowledge shall my righteous servant justify many" (Isa. 53:11). Our Lord himself puts beyond all doubt the validity of such a construction when he defines for us the purpose of his coming into the world in terms that precisely convey such a connotation: "I came down from heaven not to do my own will but the will of him that sent me" (John 6:38). And with reference even to the climactic event which is pivotal in the accomplishment of redemption, his death, he says, "On this account the Father loves me because I lay down my life in order that I may take it again. No one takes it from me, but I lay it down of myself. I have authority to lay it down, and I have authority to take it again. This commandment have I received from my Father" (John 10:17-18). And nothing to this effect could be more explicit than the words of the apostle. "For as through the disobedience of the one man many were constituted sinners, even so through the obedience of the one many will be constituted righteous" (Rom. 5:19). "He made himself of no reputation, taking the form of a servant, being made in the likeness of men. And being found in fashion as a man he humbled himself, becoming obedient unto death, even the death of the cross" (Phil. 2:7-8; *cf.* also Gal. 4:4). And the epistle to the Hebrews also has its own peculiar turn of expression when it says that the Son "learned obedience from the things which he suffered, and being made perfect became the author of eternal salvation to all them that obey him" (5:8-9; *cf.* 2:10).

This obedience has frequently been designated the active and passive obedience. This formula when properly interpreted serves the good purpose of setting forth the two distinct aspects of Christ's work of obedience. But it is necessary at the outset to relieve the formula of some of the misapprehensions and misapplications to which it is subject.[1]

(a) The term "passive obedience" does not mean that in

1. Cf. T. J. Crawford: *The Doctrine of the Holy Scripture Respecting the Atonement* (Edinburgh, 1880), pp. 58ff., 89f.; Hugh Martin: *op. cit.*, Chap. IV, especially p. 81; James M'Lagan: *Lectures and Sermons* (Aberdeen, 1853), pp. 54ff.; Francis Turretin: *op. cit.*, Loc. XIV, Q, XIII.

anything Christ did was he passive, the involuntary victim of obedience imposed upon him. It is obvious that any such conception would contradict the very notion of *obedience*. And it must be jealously maintained that even in his sufferings and death our Lord was not the passive recipient of that to which he was subjected. In his sufferings he was supremely active, and death itself did not befall him as it befalls other men. "No one takes it from me, but I lay it down of myself" are his own words. He was obedient unto death, Paul tells us. And this does not mean that his obedience extended to the threshold of death but rather that he was obedient to the extent of yielding up his spirit in death and of laying down his life. In the exercise of self-conscious sovereign volition, knowing that all things had been accomplished and that the very moment of time for the accomplishment of this event had arrived, he effected the separation of body and spirit and committed the latter to the Father. He dismissed his spirit and laid down his life. The word "passive," then, should not be interpreted to mean pure passivity in anything that came within the scope of his obedience. The sufferings he endured, sufferings which reached their climax in his death upon the accursed tree, were an integral part of his obedience and were endured in pursuance of the task given him to accomplish.

(b) Neither are we to suppose that we can allocate certain phases or acts of our Lord's life on earth to the active obedience and certain other phases and acts to the passive obedience. The distinction between the active and passive obedience is not a distinction of periods. It is our Lord's whole work of obedience in every phase and period that is described as active and passive, and we must avoid the mistake of thinking that the active obedience applies to the obedience of his life and the passive to the obedience of his final sufferings and death.

The real use and purpose of the formula is to emphasize

the two distinct aspects of our Lord's vicarious obedience. The truth expressed rests upon the recognition that the law of God has both penal sanctions and positive demands. It demands not only the full discharge of its precepts but also the infliction of penalty for all infractions and shortcomings. It is this twofold demand of the law of God which is taken into account when we speak of the active and passive obedience of Christ. Christ as the vicar of his people came under the curse and condemnation due to sin and he also fulfilled the law of God in all its positive requirements. In other words, he took care of the guilt of sin and perfectly fulfilled the demands of righteousness. He perfectly met both the penal and the preceptive requirements of God's law. The passive obedience refers to the former and the active obedience to the latter. Christ's obedience was vicarious in the bearing of the full judgment of God upon sin, and it was vicarious in the full discharge of the demands of righteousness. His obedience becomes the ground of the remission of sin and of actual justification.

We must not view this obedience in any artificial or mechanical sense. When we speak of Christ's obedience we must not think of it as consisting simply in formal fulfillment of the commandments of God. What the obedience of Christ involved for him is perhaps nowhere more strikingly expressed than in Hebrews 2:10-18; 5:8-10 where we are told that Jesus "learned obedience from the things which he suffered," that he was made perfect through sufferings, and that "being made perfect he became to all who obey him the author of eternal salvation." When we examine these passages the following lessons become apparent. (1) It was not through mere incarnation that Christ wrought our salvation and secured our redemption. (2) It was not through mere death that salvation was accomplished. (3) It was not simply through the death upon the cross that Jesus became the author of salvation. (4) The death upon the cross, as the climatic requirement of the price of redemption, was *discharged* as the supreme act of obedience; it was not death resistlessly inflicted but death upon the cross willingly and obediently wrought.

When we speak of obedience we are thinking not merely of formal acts of accomplishment but also of the disposition, will, determination, and volition which lie back of and are registered in these formal acts. And when we speak of the death of our Lord upon the cross as the supreme act of his obedience we are thinking not merely of the overt act of dying upon the tree but also of the disposition, will, and determinate volition which lay back of the overt act. And, furthermore, we are required to ask the question: whence did our Lord derive the disposition and holy determination to give up his life in death as the supreme act of self-sacrifice and obedience? We are compelled to ask this question because it was in *human nature* that he rendered this obedience and gave up his life in death. And these texts in the epistle to the Hebrews confirm not only the propriety but the necessity of this question. For in these texts we are distinctly informed that he *learned* obedience, and he learned this obedience from the things that he suffered. It was requisite that he should have been made perfect through sufferings and become the author of salvation through this perfecting. It was not, of course, a perfecting that required the sanctification from sin to holiness. He was always holy, harmless, undefiled, and separate from sinners. But there was the perfecting of development and growth in the course and path of his obedience — he *learned* obedience. The heart and mind and will of our Lord had been molded — shall we not say forged? — in the furnace of temptation and suffering. And it was in virtue of what he had learned in that experience of temptation and suffering that he was able, at the climactic point fixed by the arrangements of infallible wisdom and everlasting love, to be obedient unto death, even the death of the cross. It was only as having learned obedience in the path of inerrant and sinless discharge of the Father's will that his heart and mind and will were framed to the point of being able freely and voluntarily to yield up his life in death upon the accursed tree.

It was through this course of obedience and of learning obedience that he was made perfect as Savior, that is to say, became fully equipped so as to be constituted a perfect Savior. It was the equipment forged through all the experiences of trial, temptation, and suffering that provided the resources requisite for the climactic requirement of his commission. It was that obedience, brought to its consummate fruition on the cross, that constituted him an all-sufficient and perfect Savior. And this is just saying that it was the obedience learned and rendered through the whole course of humiliation that made him perfect as the captain of salvation. It is obedience learned through suffering, perfected through suffering, and consummated in the suffering of death upon the cross that defines his work and accomplishment as the author of salvation. It was by obedience he secured our salvation because it was by obedience he wrought the work that secured it.

Obedience, therefore, is not something that may be conceived of artificially or abstractedly. It is obedience that enlisted all the resources of his perfect humanity, obedience that resided in his person, and obedience of which he is ever the perfect embodiment. It is obedience that finds its permanent efficacy and virtue in him. And we become the beneficiaries of it, indeed the partakers of it, by union with him. It is this that serves to advertise the significance of that which is the central truth of all soteriology, namely, union and communion with Christ.

While the concept of obedience supplies us with an inclusive category in terms of which the atoning work of Christ may be viewed and which establishes at the outset the active agency of Christ in the accomplishment of redemption, we must now proceed to analyse those specific categories by means of which the Scripture sets forth the nature of the atonement.

1. *Sacrifice.* It lies on the face of the New Testament that Christ's work is construed as sacrifice.[2] And the only question is: what notion of sacrifice governs this pervasive use of the term sacrifice as it is applied to the work of Christ? This question can be answered only by determining what was the notion of sacrifice entertained by the New Testament speakers and writers. Steeped as these were in the language and ideas of the Old Testament, there is but one direction in which to seek their interpretation of the meaning and effect of sacrifice. What is the Old Testament idea of sacrifice? Much debate has revolved around this question. But we can be content to say with confidence that the Old Testament sacrifices were basically expiatory. This means that they had reference to sin and guilt. Sin involves a certain liability, a liability arising from the holiness of God, on the one hand, and the gravity of sin as the contradiction of that holiness, on the other. The sacrifice was the divinely instituted provision whereby the sin might be covered and the liability to divine wrath and curse removed. The Old Testament worshiper when he brought his oblation to the altar substituted an animal victim in his place. In laying his hands upon the head of the offering there was transferred *symbolically* to the offering the sin and liability of the offerer. This is the pivot on which the transaction turned. The notion in essence was

2. Cf. B. B. Warfield: *Biblical Doctrines* (New York, 1929), "Christ our Sacrifice," pp. 401-435; W. P. Paterson: *A Dictionary of the Bible*, ed. James Hastings (New York, 1902), Vol. IV, pp. 329-349.

that the sin of the offerer was imputed to the offering and the offering bore as a result the death-penalty. It was substitutive endurance of the penalty or liability due to sin.

Obviously there was a great disproportion between the offerer and the offering and a corresponding disproportion between the liability of the offerer and that executed upon the offering. These offerings were but shadows and patterns. Nevertheless the expiatory notion is apparent, and it is this expiatory significance that provides the background for the interpretation of Christ's sacrifice. The work of Christ is expiatory, expiatory indeed with a transcendent virtue, efficacy, and perfection that could not apply to bulls and goats, yet expiatory in terms of the pattern provided by the Old Testament sacrificial ritual. This means that to him, as the great sacrifice offered without spot to God, were transferred the sins and liabilities of those on whose behalf he offered himself as a sacrifice. By reason of this imputation he suffered and died, just for unjust, that he might bring us nigh to God. By one sacrifice he hath perfected forever all them that are sanctified.

While the New Testament writers do not find in Christ's offering of himself a literal fulfillment of all the prescriptions of the Levitical law[3] as these applied to the animal offerings, yet it is very apparent that they have distinctly before their minds certain specific transactions of the Mosaic ritual. For example, in Hebrews 9:6-15 the transactions of the great day of atonement are specifically mentioned, and it is with these transactions clearly in mind and on the basis of the symbolical and typical import of this ritual that the writer sets forth the transcendent efficacy, perfection, and finality of the sacrifice of Christ. "But Christ having come a high priest of the good things to come, through the greater and more perfect

---

3. *Cf.* James Denney: *The Death of Christ* (New York, 1903), pp. 54f.

tabernacle, not made with hands, that is to say, not of this creation, nor yet through the blood of goats and calves, but through his own blood, he entered in once for all into the holy place, having obtained eternal redemption" (vers. 11-12; cf. vers. 23-24).

Likewise in Hebrews 13:10-13 we cannot fail to see that the writer exhibits the work of Christ and his sacrifice under the form of those sin-offerings — the sin-offering for the priest and the sin-offering for the whole congregation — whose blood was brought into the holy place and whose flesh and skin and legs were burned without the camp. Since no part of the flesh of such sin-offerings was available for the priests, the writer applies this to Christ, not indeed with literal fulfillment of all the details but with appreciation of the parabolic and typical significance. "Wherefore Jesus also, in order that he might sanctify the people through his own blood, suffered without the gate. Let us go forth therefore unto him without the camp, bearing his reproach" (vers. 12-13).

Jesus, therefore, offered himself a sacrifice and that most particularly under the form or pattern supplied by the sin-offering of the Levitical economy. In thus offering himself he expiated guilt and purged away sin so that we may draw near to God in full assurance of faith and enter into the holiest by the blood of Jesus, having our hearts sprinkled from an evil conscience and our bodies washed with pure water.

In this connection we must also keep in view what we have reflected on already that the Levitical sacrifices were patterned after the heavenly exemplar, after what the epistle to the Hebrews calls "the heavenly things." The bloody offerings of the Mosaic ritual were patterns of the grand offerings of Christ himself by which the things in the heavens were purified (Heb. 9:23). This serves to confirm the thesis that what was constitutive in the Levitical sacrifices must also have been constitutive in the sacrifice of Christ. If the

Levitical sacrifices were expiatory, how much more must the archetypal offering have been expiatory, and expiatory, be it remembered, not on the plane of the temporary, provisional, preparatory, and partial but on the plane of the eternal, the permanently real, the final, and the complete. The archetypal offering was therefore efficacious in a way that the ectypal could not be. It is this thought that is in evidence when we read, "How much more shall the blood of Christ, who through the eternal spirit offered himself without spot to God, purge our conscience from dead works to serve the living God" (Heb. 9:14). We must interpret the sacrifice of Christ in terms of the Levitical patterns because they were themselves patterned after Christ's offering. But it is just because the Levitical were only patterns that we must also recognize the limitations by which they were encompassed in contrast with the perfect character of Christ's own offering. And it is because such limitations inhered in the Levitical offerings that we do not find and could not expect to find in the sacrifice of Christ a literal fulfillment of all the details of the Levitical sacrifices. It was the disproportion between the offerer and the offering and between the liability of the offerer and the shedding of the blood of the offering under the Old Testament ritual that made necessary the elimination of all such disproportion in the case of Christ's sacrifice. The absence of this disproportion in the sacrifice of the Son of God is correlative with the absence in his case of all the details of Levitical prescription which would have been incompatible with the unique and transcendent character of his self-oblation.

That Christ's work was to offer himself a sacrifice for sin implies, however, a complementary truth too frequently overlooked. It is that, if Christ offered himself as a sacrifice, he was also a priest.[4] And it was as a priest that he offered

---

4. *Cf.* Hugh Martin: *op. cit.*, Chap. III.

himself. He was not offered up by another; he offered himself. This is something that could not be exemplified in the ritual of the Old Testament. The priest did not offer himself and neither did the offering offer itself. But in Christ we have this unique combination that serves to exhibit the uniqueness of his sacrifice, the transcendent character of his priestly office, and the perfection inherent in his priestly offering. It is in virtue of his priestly office and in pursuance of his priestly function that he makes atonement for sin. He indeed was the lamb slain, but he was also the priest that offered himself as the lamb of God to take away the sin of the world. It is this amazing conjuncture that the union in him of priestly office and piacular offering evinces. It is all implied in the simple expression we so often quote but seldom appreciate, "he offered himself without spot to God." And it verifies to the fullest extent, what we found already, that in the climactic event which registered and brought to completion his sacrificial act he was intensely active, and active, be it remembered, in offering to God the oblation that expiated the full toll of divine condemnation against a multitude whom no man can number out of every nation and kindred and people and tongue.

Furthermore and finally, it is the recognition of Christ's priestly function that ties up the sacrifice once offered with the abiding priestly function of the Redeemer. He is a priest for ever after the order of Melchizedek. He is a priest now, not to offer sacrifice but as the permanent personal embodiment of all the efficacy and virtue that accrued from the sacrifice once offered. And it is as such he ever continues to make intercession for his people. His ever-continuing and always-prevailing intercession is bound to the sacrifice once offered. But it is thus bound because it is in his capacity as the great high priest of our profession that he perfected the one and continues the other.

2. *Propitiation.* The Greek word which stands for our English word "propitiation" does not appear frequently in the New Testament. This may seem surprising when we consider that it occurs with such frequency in the Greek version of the Old Testament, the word so often translated by our English word "atonement." We might think that a word which is so common in the Greek Old Testament in connection with the ritual of expiation would have been freely used by the writers of the New Testament. But this is not the case.

This fact does not mean, however, that the atoning work of Christ is not to be interpreted in terms of propitiation.[5] There are passages in which the language of propitiation is expressly applied to the work of Christ (Rom. 3:25; Heb. 2:17; 1 John 2:2; 4:10). And this means, without question, that the work of Christ is to be construed as propitiation. But there is also another consideration. The frequency with which the concept appears in the Old Testament in connection with the sacrificial ritual, the fact that the New Testament applies to the work of Christ the very term which denoted this concept in the Greek Old Testament, and the fact that the New Testament regards the Levitical ritual as providing the pattern for the sacrifice of Christ lead to the conclusion that this is a category in terms of which the sacrifice of Christ is not only properly but necessarily interpreted. In other words, the idea of propitiation is so woven into the fabric of the Old Testament ritual that it would be impossible to regard that ritual as the pattern of the sacrifice of Christ if propitiation did not occupy a similar place in the one great sacrifice once offered. This is but another way of saying that sacrifice and propi-

5. *Cf.* T. J. Crawford: *op. cit.*, pp. 77ff.; George Smeaton: *The Doctrine of the Atonement as Taught by the Apostles* (Edinburgh, 1870), pp. 137ff.; A. A. Hodge: *The Atonement* (Philadelphia, 1867), pp. 39f., 179ff. Most recently see the careful and detailed study by Roger R. Nicole: "C. H. Dodd and the Doctrine of Propitiation" in *The Westminster Theological Journal*, May 1955, Vol. XVII, 2, pp. 117-157.

tiation stand in the closest relations with one another. The express application of the term "propitiation" to the work of Christ by the New Testament writers is the confirmation of this conclusion.

But what does propitiation mean? In the Hebrew of the Old Testament it is expressed by a word which means to "cover." In connection with this covering there are, in particular, three things to be noted: (1) it is in reference to sin that the covering takes place; (2) the effect of this covering is cleansing and forgiveness; (3) it is before the Lord that both the covering and its effect take place (cf. especially Lev. 4:35; 10:17; 16:30). This means that sin creates a situation *in relation to the Lord*, a situation that makes the covering necessary. It is this Godward reference of both the sin and the covering that must be fully appreciated. It may be said that the sin, or perhaps the person who has sinned, is covered before the sight of the Lord. In the thought of the Old Testament there is but one construction that we can place upon this provision of the sacrificial ritual. It is that sin evokes the holy displeasure or wrath of God. Vengeance is the reaction of the holiness of God to sin, and the covering is that which provides for the removal of divine displeasure which the sin evokes. It is obvious that we are brought to the threshold of that which is clearly denoted by the Greek rendering in both Old and New Testaments, namely, that of propitiation. To propitiate means to "placate," "pacify," "appease," "conciliate." And it is this idea that is applied to the atonement accomplished by Christ.

Propitiation presupposes the wrath and displeasure of God, and the purpose of propitiation is the removal of this displeasure. Very simply stated the doctrine of propitiation means that Christ propitiated the wrath of God and rendered God propitious to his people.

Perhaps no tenet respecting the atonement has been

more violently criticized than this one.[6] It has been assailed as involving a mythological conception of God, as supposing internal conflict in the mind of God and between the persons of the Godhead. It has been charged that this doctrine represents the Son as winning over the incensed Father to clemency and love, a supposition wholly inconsistent with the fact that the love of God is the very fount from which the atonement springs.

When the doctrine of propitiation is presented in this light it can be very effectively criticized and can be exposed as a revolting caricature of the Christian gospel. But the doctrine of propitiation does not involve this caricature by which it has been misconceived and misrepresented. To say the least, this kind of criticism has failed to understand or appreciate some elementary and important distinctions.

First of all, to love and to be propitious are not convertible terms. It is false to suppose that the doctrine of propitiation regards propitiation as that which causes or constrains the divine love. It is loose thinking of a deplorable sort to claim that propitiation of the divine wrath does prejudice to or is incompatible with the fullest recognition that the atonement is the provision of the divine love.

Secondly, propitiation is not a turning of the wrath of God into love. The propitiation of the divine wrath, effected in the expiatory work of Christ, is the provision of God's eternal and unchangeable love, so that through the propitiation of his own wrath that love may realize its purpose in a way that is consonant with and to the glory of the dictates of his holiness. It is one thing to say that the wrathful God is

6. Cf. Auguste Sabatier: *The Doctrine of the Atonement and Its Historical Evolution* (Eng. Trans. New York, 1904), pp. 29, 113, 118ff.; F. D. Maurice: *The Doctrine of Sacrifice Deduced from the Scriptures* (London, 1893). pp. 152f., 157ff.; D. M. Baillie: *God Was in Christ* (New York, 1948), pp. 186ff.; Hastings Rashdall: *The Idea of the Atonement in Christian Theology* (London, 1925), pp. 100f.

made loving. That would be entirely false. It is another thing to say the wrathful God is loving. That is profoundly true. But it is also true that the wrath by which he is wrathful is propitiated through the cross. This propitiation is the fruit of the divine love that provided it. "Herein is love, not that we loved God, but that he loved us and sent his Son to be the propitiation for our sins" (1 John 4:10). The propitiation is the ground upon which the divine love operates and the channel through which it flows in achieving its end.

Thirdly, propitiation does not detract from the love and mercy of God; it rather enhances the marvel of his love. For it shows the cost that redemptive love entails. God is love. But the supreme object of that love is himself. And because he loves himself supremely he cannot suffer what belongs to the integrity of his character and glory to be compromised or curtailed. That is the reason for the propitiation. God appeases his own holy wrath in the cross of Christ in order that the purpose of his love to lost men may be accomplished in accordance with and to the vindication of all the perfections that constitute his glory. "Whom God hath set forth to be a propitiation through faith in his blood to show his righteousness ... that he might himself be just, and the justifier of him that hath faith in Jesus" (Rom. 3:25-26).

The antipathy to the doctrine of propitiation as the propitiating of divine wrath rests, however, upon failure to appreciate what the atonement is. The atonement is that which meets the exigencies of holiness and justice. The wrath of God is the inevitable reaction of the divine holiness against sin. Sin is the contradiction of the perfection of God and he cannot but recoil against that which is the contradiction of himself. Such recoil is his holy indignation. "The wrath of God is revealed from heaven against all ungodliness and unrighteousness of men who hold the truth in unrighteousness (Rom. 1:18). The judgment of God upon sin is essentially his wrath. If we are to believe that the atonement is God's vicarious dealing with the judgment upon sin, it is absolutely necessary to hold that it is the vicarious endurance of that in which this judgment is epitomized. To deny propitiation is to undermine the nature of the atonement as the vicarious endurance of the penalty of sin. In a word, it is to deny substitutionary atonement. To glory in the cross is to glory in Christ as the propitiatory sacrifice once offered, as the abiding propitiatory, and as the one who embodies in himself for ever all the propitiatory efficacy of the propitiation once for all accomplished. "And if any one sin, we have an advocate with the Father, Jesus Christ the righteous. And he is the propitiation for our sins (and not for ours only but also for the whole world" (1 John 2:1-2).

3. *Reconciliation.* Propitiation places in the focus of attention the wrath of God and the divine provision for the removal of that wrath. Reconciliation places in the focus of attention our alienation from God and the divine method of restoring us to his favor. Obviously these two aspects of the work of Christ are closely related. But the distinction is important. Only by observing the distinction can we discover the riches of the divine provision to meet the necessities of our manifold need.

Reconciliation presupposes disrupted relations between God and men. It implies enmity and alienation. This alienation is twofold, our alienation from God and God's alienation from us. The cause of the alienation is, of course, our sin, but the alienation consists not only in our unholy enmity against God but also in God's holy alienation from us. Our iniquities have separated between us and our God and our sins have hid his face (cf. Isa. 59:2). If we dissociate from the word "enmity" as applied to God everything of the nature of malice and malignity, we may properly speak of this alienation on the part of God as his holy enmity towards us. It is this alienation that the reconciliation contemplates and removes.

We might be ready to think that the reconciliation terminates not only God's holy enmity against us but upon our unholy enmity towards him. Our English word would quite readily create this impression. This notion, furthermore, would appear to be supported by the usage of the New Testament itself. It is never said in so many words that God is reconciled to us but rather that we are reconciled to God (Rom. 5:10-11; 2 Cor. 5:20). And when the active voice is used, God is spoken of as reconciling us to himself (2 Cor. 5:18-19; Eph. 2:16; Col. 1:20-21). This would seem to clinch the argument that the reconciliation terminates upon our enmity against God and not upon his holy alienation from us. And so it has been maintained that when the reconciliation is conceived as action on the part of God it is that which God has done to turn our enmity into love and when it is conceived as result it is the putting away of our enmity against God. Consequently the reconciliation has been construed as consisting in that which God has done so that our enmity may be removed. In a word, the thought is focused on our enmity, and the doctrine of reconciliation is constructed in these terms.[7]

When we examine the Scripture more closely we shall find the reverse to be the case. It is not our enmity against God that comes to the forefront in the reconciliation but God's alienation from us. This alienation on the part of God arises indeed from our sin; it is our sin that evokes this reaction of his holiness. But it is God's alienation from us that is brought into the foreground whether the reconciliation is viewed as action or as result.

7. Cf. A. W. Argyle: "The New Testament Interpretation of the Death of our Lord" in The Expository Times (June, 1949), p. 255; G. C. Workman: At Onement or Reconciliation with God (New York, 1911), pp. 76ff.; F. W. Dillistone: The Significance of the Cross (Philadelphia, 1944), pp. 114ff.; John B. Champion: The Heart of the New Testament (Grand Rapids, 1941), pp. 21ff.

It is instructive in this regard to examine a few instances of the occurrence of the word "reconcile" in the New Testament. These instances apply to the use of the word in human relations. The first is Matthew 5:23-24.[8] "If therefore thou offerest thy gift at the altar and there rememberest that thy brother hath something against thee, leave there thy gift before the altar and go thy way, first be reconciled to thy brother, and then come and offer thy gift." Here it is the meaning of the imperative "be reconciled to thy brother" that is our present interest. The following observations require to be mentioned.

(a) It is not assumed or suggested that the worshiper who is offering his gift at the altar entertains any malice or enmity in his heart against the brother to whom he is to be reconciled. That might be or it might not be. But there is no intrusion of such a factor into the situation. The factor that is given as the reason for the interruption in the act of worship is simply that there is alienation. Something has entered into the relations of the two persons which the person called the brother considers to be a grievance against the person bringing the gift to the altar, something which the former considers to be a culpable breach of harmonious relations on the part of the latter.

(b) It is probably assumed in this case that the worshiper has done something to wrong the other brother, that he is guilty of some misdemeanor or breach of love. However, this is not absolutely necessary, and whether this be true or not we have to take account of the fact that what the worshiper is commanded to do he is required to do irrespective of the justice or injustice of the brother's thought and judgment.

(c) What the worshiper is commanded to do is to be reconciled to the brother. The command "be reconciled" does

8. *Cf.* T. J. Crawford: *op. cit.*, pp. 69ff.

not mean "put away your enmity or malice." He is not assumed to entertain any malice. Besides, if that is what he is commanded to do, he would not need to leave the altar to do it. He could not be in a better place than in the sanctuary if what he is required to do is to repent and put away his ill will. What the worshiper is commanded to do is something quite different. He is required to leave the altar, to repair to his offended brother, and then to do something. What is it? It is to remove the ground of estrangement or alienation on the part of the brother. Put things right with the brother so that he will not have any reason for grievance; do what is necessary so that there may be the resumption of harmonious relations. The reconciliation as act consists in the removal of the ground of disharmony; the reconciliation as result is the resumption of relations of harmony, understanding, and peace.

It is all-important to recognize, therefore, that what the worshiper takes into account in the act of reconciliation is the grievance entertained by the brother; it is the frame of mind of the person to whom he is reconciled that he is to consider and not any enmity which he himself entertains. And, if we use the word "enmity," it is the enmity on the part of the offended brother that is brought into the forefront of thought and consideration. In other words, it is the "against" entertained by the offended brother that the reconciliation has in view; the reconciliation effects the removal of this "against."

This passage then provides us with a most instructive lesson regarding the meaning of "be reconciled"; it shows that this expression, in this instance at least, focuses thought and consideration not upon the enmity of the person who is said to be reconciled but upon the alienation in the mind of the person with whom the reconciliation is made. And, if the meaning which obtains in this passage is that which holds in connection with our reconciliation to God through the death of Christ, then what is thrust into the foreground when we are said to be reconciled to God is the alienation of God from us, the holy enmity on the part of God by which we are alienated from him. The reconciliation as action would be the removal of the ground of God's alienation from us; the reconciliation as result would be the harmonious and peaceful relation established because the ground of God's alienation from us had been removed. At this stage we could not affirm that this is the precise force of the word "reconciliation" in reference to our reconciliation with God. We shall have to derive our doctrine of reconciliation from the passages which deal specifically with that subject. But Matthew 5:23-24 does show us that in the usage of the New Testament the word "reconcile" is used in a sense very different from that which might readily be suggested by our English word. Hence when the New Testament speaks of our being reconciled to God by the death of his Son or of God's reconciling us to himself we are not to assume that the concept is to be construed in terms of the removal of our enmity against God. To say the least, Matthew 5:23-24 suggests a very different direction of thought.

Another instance of the use of the word "reconcile" which evinces the same line of thought is 1 Corinthians 7:11. Referring to the woman separated from her husband Paul says, "Let her remain unmarried or be reconciled to her husband." In this case, to whatever extent subjective enmity on the part of the woman may have entered in to cause the separation that is envisaged, it is obvious that the command to "be reconciled to her husband" cannot consist in putting away her subjective enmity or hostility. That would not bring the exhortation into effect. The reconciliation contemplates, rather, the termination of the separation and re-entrance upon proper and harmonious matrimonial relations. The reconciliation regarded as action is to cause to cease the separation and as effect the resumption of peaceful marital relations.

Again in Romans 11:15 we have an instance of the substantive "reconciliation." "For if the casting away of them is the reconciling of the world, what shall the receiving of them be but life from the dead?" It is apparent that the reconciling is contrasted with the casting away and the casting away is contrasted with the receiving. The receiving is nothing else than the reception of Israel again into divine favor and the blessing of the gospel. The casting away is the rejection of Israel from divine favor and gospel grace. The reconciling of the Gentiles, which is upon the occasion of the rejection of Israel, is, in like manner, the receiving of the Gentiles into divine favor. The reconciliation of the Gentiles, therefore, cannot be construed in terms of the putting away of enmity on the part of the Gentiles but in terms of the change in God's economy of grace when the alienation of the Gentiles came to an end and they were made fellow-citizens with the saints and of the household of God (cf. Eph. 2:11-22). To whatever extent the change from enmity to faith and love in the hearts of the Gentiles may be taken into account as the effect of the change in God's economy of grace and of judgment, grace to the Gentiles and judgment upon Israel, we must regard the "reconciliation of the world" as consisting in the change of *relation* which God sustained to the Gentile world, the change from alienation to gospel favor and blessing. It is the relationship of God to the Gentiles that is brought into the forefront in this use of the word "reconciliation."

When we proceed to deal with the passages which directly concern the work of reconciliation wrought by Christ, it is necessary for us to bear in mind that reconciliation in these other instances does not refer to the putting away of the subjective enmity in the heart of the person said to be reconciled but to the alienation on the part of the person to whom we are said to be reconciled. We shall see how it is this notion that applies to the reconciliation accomplished by Christ. The reconciliation deals with the alienation of God from us on account of our sin; by taking away sin reconciliation removes the ground of this alienation, and peace with God is the effect. The two passages which we shall consider are Romans 5:8-11; 2 Corinthians 5:18-21.

Romans 5:8-11. At the very outset the way in which the subject of reconciliation is introduced here points us to the direction in which we are to discover the meaning of reconciliation. "But God commendeth his own love toward us, in that while we were yet sinners Christ died for us" (ver. 8). The death of Christ as that which wrought reconciliation is set forth as the supreme manifestation of the love of God toward men. What is given the prominence is the love of God as it expresses itself in an action so well defined as the death of Christ. Our attention is therefore drawn, not to the subjective realm of man's attitude to God, but to the divine attitude as it is demonstrated in an historical event. To interpret the reconciliation in terms of what occurs in our subjective disposition would interfere with this orientation. But there are also more directly confirmatory reasons for thinking thus.

(a) Paul tells us expressly that we were reconciled to God through the death of his Son. The tense indicates that it is an accomplished fact, wrought once for all when Christ died. We can see how impossible it is to interpret the reconciliation as God's removal of our enmity or as the laying aside of enmity on our part. It is true that God did something once for all to insure that our enmity would be removed and that we would be induced to lay aside our enmity. But then that which God did once for all would not consist in the removal of our enmity or in the putting away of our enmity. Furthermore, the *a fortiori* argument which Paul uses in this passage would supply us with an incongruous construction if we were to regard the reconciliation as the removal on God's part or the laying aside on our part of our enmity. The argument would have to run in some such way as follows: "For if when we were enemies we laid aside our enmity against God through the death of his Son, how much more, having laid aside our enmity, shall we be saved by his life" (cf. ver. 10). The incoherence is apparent and can only be remedied by placing upon the word "reconcile" a very different meaning.

(b) The words, "reconciled to God through the death of his Son" (ver. 10) are parallel to the words "justified now in his blood" (ver. 9). Such parallelism is presupposed in the sequence of the argument. But justification is always forensic and does not refer to any subjective change in man's disposition. Since this is so, the expression that is parallel to it, namely, "reconciled to God" must be given a similarly juridical force and can only mean that which came to pass in the objective sphere of the divine action and judgment.

(c) The reconciliation is something received — "we have received the reconciliation" (ver. 11). To say the least, it is most unreasonable to try to adjust or accommodate this notion to the idea of the removal or the laying aside of our enmity. The concept here is one in which something is represented as made over to us as a free gift. It is, of course, true that it is by the work of God's grace in us that we are enabled to turn from enmity against God to faith, repentance, and love. But in the language of Scripture this latter work of grace is not represented in such terms as are used here. We can detect the inappropriateness of such a rendering if we try to paraphrase with such a conception in mind: "we have now received the removal of our enmity" or "we have now received the laying aside of our enmity." On the other hand, if we regard the reconciliation as the free grace of God in the removal of alienation from God and acceptance into his favor, then it all becomes coherent and meaningful. What we have received is reinstatement in the favor of God. How consistent with the terms of the passage and with the rejoicing of the apostle to say, "We joy in God through our Lord Jesus Christ through whom now we no longer suffer alienation from God but have been received into favor and peace with him."

(d) Paul says that it was while we were yet enemies that we were reconciled to God through the death of his Son (ver. 10). It is altogether feasible to regard the word "enemies" here as reflecting not upon our enmity against God but as referring to the alienation from God to which we had been subjected. The same word is used in this passive sense in Romans 11:28. If this sense is adopted the antithesis instituted between enmity and reconciliation is exactly that between alienation and reception into divine favor. This would corroborate the foregoing argument as to the meaning of reconciliation. But even if the word "enemies" be understood in the active sense of our hostility to God, the same sense of reconciliation would have to be maintained. How could any other interpretation comport with the argument of the apostle? It could scarcely be said, "If, being active enemies of God, our enmity was removed by the death of his Son, how much more having had our enmity removed, shall we be saved by his life."

2 Corinthians 5:18-21. It will serve to confirm what we have found in Romans 5:8-11 to set forth the salient features of the teaching of this passage.

(a) The reconciliation is represented as a work of God. It begins with God and it is accomplished by him. "All things are of God who reconciled us to himself" (ver. 18). "God was in Christ reconciling the world to himself" (ver. 19). This emphasis upon divine monergism advises us that reconciliation is a work that does not, as such, draw within its scope human action. As accomplishment it does not enlist, nor is it dependent upon, the activity of men.

(b) Reconciliation is a finished work. The tenses in verses 18, 19, 21 put this beyond doubt. It is not a work being continuously wrought by God; it is something accomplished in the past. God is not only the sole agent but also the agent of action already perfected.

(c) That in which the reconciliation consisted is expounded for us in this passage. "Him who knew no sin he made to be sin for us, that we might become the righteousness of God in him" (ver. 21). This clearly points us to the vicarious sin-bearing of Christ as that which brought the reconciliation into being. This forensic character of the reconciliation is also borne out in verse 19 where "not reckoning to them their trespasses" is related to the reconciling of the world as the explanation of that in which the reconciliation consists or as the consequence in which it issues. In either case reconciliation has its affinities with the non-imputation of trespasses rather than with any subjective operation.

(d) This accomplished work of reconciliation is the message committed to the messengers of the gospel (ver. 19). It constitutes the content of the message. But the message is that which is declared to be a fact. Conversion, it ought to be remembered, is not the gospel. It is the demand of the gospel message and the proper response to it. Any transformation which occurs in us is the effect in us of that which is proclaimed to have been accomplished by God. The change in our hearts and minds presupposes the reconciliation.

(e) The exhortation "be ye reconciled to God" (ver. 20) should be interpreted in terms of what we have found to be the ruling conception in reconciliation. It means: be no longer in a state of alienation from God but enter rather into the relation of favor and peace established by the reconciliatory work of Christ. Take advantage of the grace of God and enter into this status of peace with God through our Lord Jesus Christ.

The reconciliation of which the Scripture speaks, as accomplished by the death of Christ, contemplates, therefore, the relation of God to us. It presupposes a relation of alienation and it effects a relation of favor and peace. This new relation is constituted by the removal of the ground for the alienation. The ground is sin and guilt. The removal is wrought in the vicarious work of Christ, when he was made sin for us that we might become the righteousness of God in him. Christ took upon himself the sin and guilt, the condemnation and the curse of those on whose behalf he died. This is the epitome of divine grace and love. It is God's own provision and it is his accomplishment. God himself in his own Son has removed the ground of offence and we receive the reconciliation. It is the message of this divine performance, perfected and complete, that is addressed to us in the gospel, and the demand of faith is crystallized in the plea that is uttered on behalf of Christ and as of God, "be ye reconciled to God." Believe that the message is one of fact and enter into the joy and blessing of what God has wrought. Receive the reconciliation.

4. *Redemption.*[9] The idea of redemption must not be reduced to the general notion of deliverance. The language of redemption is the language of purchase and more specifically of ransom. And ransom is the securing of a release by the payment of a price. The evidence that establishes this concept of redemption is very copious, and no doubt need remain that the redemption secured by Christ is to be interpreted in such terms. The word of our Lord himself (Matt. 20:28; Mark 10:45) should place beyond all doubt three facts: (1) that the work he came into the world to accomplish is a work of ransom, (2) that the giving of his life was the ransom price, and (3) that this ransom was substitutionary in its nature.

9. *Cf.* B. B. Warfield: *op. cit.*, pp. 327-398; T. J. Crawford: *op. cit.* pp. 60ff.

Ransom presupposes some kind of bondage or captivity, and redemption, therefore, implies that from which the ransom secures us. Just as sacrifice is directed to the need created by our guilt, propitiation to the need that arises from the wrath of God, and reconciliation to the need arising from our alienation from God, so redemption is directed to the bondage to which our sin has consigned us. This bondage is, of course, multiform. Consequently redemption as purchase or ransom receives a wide variety of reference and application. Redemption applies to every respect in which we are bound, and it releases us unto a liberty that is nothing less than the liberty of the glory of the children of God.

We must not, of course, press the language of purchase or ransom unduly. As T. J. Crawford reminds us, we may not attempt "to trace in the work of Christ an exact conformity to everything that is done in human acts of redemption."[10] Our constructions would thus become artificial and fanciful. But that "our salvation is accomplished by *a process of commutation analogous to the payment of a ransom*" (*ibid.* p. 63) lies on the face of the New Testament. From what aspects then does the Scripture view the redemption wrought by Christ? The most apparent of these may be comprehended under the two following divisions.

(i) *Law.* When the Scripture relates redemption to the law of God, the terms it uses are to be carefully marked. It does not say that we are redeemed from the law. That would not be an accurate description and the Scripture refrains from such an expression. We are not redeemed from the obligation to love the Lord our God with all our heart and soul and strength and mind and our neighbor as ourselves. The law is comprehended in these two commandments (Matt. 22:40)

10. *Op. cit.*, p. 62.

and love is the fulfilling of the law (Rom. 13:10). To suppose that we are delivered from the law in the sense of such obligation would bring contradiction into the design of Christ's work. It would contradict the very nature of God to think that any person can ever be relieved of the necessity to love God with the whole heart and to obey his commandments. When Scripture relates redemption to the law of God it uses terms that are more specific.

(a) *The curse of the law.* "Christ hath redeemed us from the curse of the law, being made a curse for us" (Gal. 3:13). The curse of the law is its penal sanction. This is essentially the wrath or curse of God, the displeasure which rests upon every infraction of the law's demand. "Cursed is every one that continueth not in all things written in the book of the law to do them" (Gal. 3:10). Without deliverance from this curse there could be no salvation. It is from this curse that Christ has purchased his people and the price of the purchase was that he himself became a curse. He became so identified with the curse resting upon his people that the whole of it in all its unrelieved intensity became his. That curse he bore and that curse he exhausted. That was the price paid for this redemption and the liberty secured for the beneficiaries is that there is no more curse.

(b) *The ceremonial law.* "When the fulness of the time came, God sent forth his Son, made of a woman, made under law, in order that he might redeem them that were under the law, that we might receive the adoption of sons" (Gal. 4:4-5). What is in view here is redemption from the tutelary bondage of the Mosaic economy.[11] The people of God under the Old Testament were children of God by the divine adoption of grace. But they were as children under age, under tutors and governors until the time appointed of the father (*cf.* Gal.

11. *Cf.* John Calvin: *ad loc.*

4:2). Of this tutelary, pedagogical discipline the Mosaic economy was the minister (cf. Gal. 3:23-24). Paul is contrasting this period of tutelage under the Mosaic law with the full liberty bestowed upon all believers, whether Jews or Gentiles, under the gospel. This full liberty and privilege he calls the adoption of sons (Gal. 4:5). Christ came in order that this adoption might be secured. The consideration particularly relevant to the price paid for this redemption is the fact that Christ was made under law. He was born under the Mosaic law; he was subjected to its conditions and he fulfilled its terms. In him the Mosaic law realized its purpose, and its meaning received in him its permanent validity and embodiment. Consequently he redeemed from the relative and privisional bondage of which the Mosaic economy was the instrument.

This redemption has significance not only for Jews but also for Gentiles. In the gospel economy not even Gentiles are required to undergo the tutelary discipline to which Israel was subjected. "But now that faith is come we are no longer under a tutor. For we are all sons of God through faith in Christ Jesus" (Gal. 3:25-26). This great grace, that all without distinction or discrimination are sons of God by faith of Christ Jesus, is the fruit of a redemption secured by the fact that Christ was made under the Mosaic law and fulfilled its terms and purpose.

(c) *The law of works.* Christ has redeemed us from the necessity of keeping the law *as the condition of our justification and acceptance with God.* Without such redemption there could be no justification and no salvation. It is the obedience of Christ himself that has secured this release. For it is by his obedience that many will be constituted righteous (Rom. 5:19). In other words, it is the active and passive obedience of Christ that is the price of this redemption, active and passive obedience because he was made under law, fulfilled all the requirements of righteousness, and met all the sanctions of justice.

(ii) *Sin*. That Christ redeemed his people from sin follows from what has been said respecting law. The strength of sin is the law and where no law is there is no transgression (I Cor. 15:56; Rom. 4:15). But the Scripture also brings redemption into direct relation to sin. It is in this connection that the blood of Christ is clearly indicated to be the means whereby such redemption is secured. Redemption from sin embraces the several aspects from which sin may be viewed. It is redemption from sin in all its aspects and consequences. This is particularly apparent in such passages as Hebrews 9:12; Revelation 5:9. The inclusive character of redemption as it affects sin and its accompanying evils is shown perhaps most clearly by the fact that the eschatological consummation of the whole redemptive process is referred to as the redemption (cf. Luke 21:28; Rom. 8:23; Eph. 1:14; 4:30; and possibly I Cor. 1:30). That the concept of redemption should be used to designate the complete and final deliverance from all evil and the realization of the goal to which the whole process of redemptive grace moves advertises very conspicuously how closely bound up with redemption as wrought by Christ is the attainment of the liberty of the glory of the children of God. And it also shows that redemption is constitutive of the very notion of consummated bliss for the people of God. No wonder then that Old Testament prophecy should be in these terms (cf. Hosea 13:14) and that the song of the glorified should be the song of redemption (cf. Rev. 1:5-6; 5:9).

In this discussion we are thinking, however, of redemption as a finished accomplishment on the part of Christ. When redemption is viewed in that more restricted sense there are two aspects of sin which come into distinct prominence as those upon which the redemptive accomplishment of Christ bears. They are the *guilt* and the *power* of sin. And the two effects issuing from this redemptive accomplishment are respectively: (1) justification and forgiveness of sin and

(2) deliverance from the enslaving defilement and power of sin. Redemption as it affects guilt and issues in justification and remission is in view in such passages as Romans 3:24; Ephesians 1:7; Colossians 1:14; Hebrews 9:15. And redemption as it affects the enslaving power and defilement of sin is in view in Titus 2:14; 1 Peter 1:18, though in these latter we cannot exclude all forensic import.

In connection with redemption from the guilt of sin the blood of Christ as substitutionary ransom and as the ransom price of our release is brought distinctly into view. The ransom utterances of our Lord (Matt. 20:28; Mark 10:45) show beyond question that he interpreted the purpose of his coming into the world in terms of substitutionary ransom and that this ransom was nothing less than the giving of his life. And, in the usage of the New Testament, the giving of his life is the same as the shedding of his blood. Redemption, therefore, in our Lord's view consisted in substitutionary blood-shedding or blood-shedding in the room and stead of many with the end in view of thereby purchasing to himself the many on whose behalf he gave his life a ransom. It is this same notion that is reproduced in the apostolic teaching. Although the terminology is not precisely that of redemption, we cannot mistake the redemptive import of Paul's statement in his charge to the elders of Ephesus when he refers "to the church of God, which he hath purchased through his own blood" (Acts 20:28). Elsewhere the thought of Paul here is expressed overtly in the language of redemption or ransom when of Christ Jesus he says that "he gave himself on our behalf in order that he might ransom us from all iniquity and purify to himself a people for his own possession, zealous of good works" (Titus 2:14). Or again, when Paul says that in the beloved "we have redemption through his blood, the forgiveness of trespasses" (Eph. 1:7; cf. Col. 1:14), it is quite plain that he conceives of the forgiveness of sins as the blessing accrued from blood redemption. And though Hebrews 9:15 is difficult to exegete yet it is clear that the death of Christ is the means of redemption in reference to sins committed under the old covenant: the death of Christ is *redemptively* efficacious in reference to sin.

We may not artificially separate redemption as ransom from the guilt of sin from the other categories in which the work of Christ is to be interpreted. These categories are but aspects from which the work of Christ once for all accomplished must be viewed and therefore they may be said to interpermeate one another. This fact as it applies to redemption appears, for example, in Romans 3:24-26. "Being justified freely," Paul says, "by his grace through the redemption which is in Christ Jesus: whom God hath set forth a propitiation through faith in his blood . . . to show forth his righteousness at the present time, in order that he might be just and the justifier of him who is of the faith of Jesus." Here not only are redemption and propitiation collocated but there is a combination of concepts bearing upon the intent and effect of Christ's work, and this shows how closely interrelated these various concepts are. This passage exemplifies and confirms what other considerations establish, namely, that redemption from the guilt of sin must be construed in juridical terms analogous to those which must be applied to expiation, propitiation, and reconciliation.

Redemption from the *power* of sin may be called the triumphal aspect of redemption. In his finished work Christ did something once for all respecting the power of sin and it is in virtue of this victory which he secured that the power of sin is broken in all those who are united to him. It is in this connection that a strand of New Testament teaching needs to be appreciated but which is frequently overlooked. It is that not only is Christ regarded as having died for the believer but the believer is represented as having died in Christ and as having been raised up with him to newness of life. This is the result of union with Christ. For by this union Christ is not only united to those who have been given to him but they are united with him. Hence not only did Christ die for them but they died in him and rose with him (*cf.* Rom. 6:1-10; 2 Cor. 5:14-15; Eph. 2:1-7; Col. 3:1-4; 1 Pet. 4:1-2). It is this fact of having died with Christ in the efficacy of his death and of having risen with him in the power of his resurrection that insures for all the people of God deliverance from the dominion of sin. It supplies the ground for the exhortation, "Even so reckon ye yourselves to be dead indeed to sin but alive to God in Christ Jesus" (Rom. 6:11) and gives force to the apodictic assurance, "Sin shall not have dominion over you" (Rom. 6:14). It is this fact of having died and risen with Christ, viewed as an implication of the death and resurrection of Christ once for all accomplished, that provides the basis of the sanctifying process. And it is constantly pleaded as the urge and incentive to sanctification in the practice of the believer.

It is here also that we may properly reflect upon the bearing of redemption upon Satan. It is to the triumphal aspect of redemption that this is to be allocated. The early fathers of the Christian church gave a prominent place to this phase of redemption and construed it in terms of ransom paid to the devil. Such a construction became fanciful and ludicrous. Its falsity was effectively exposed by Anselm in his epochal work, *Cur Deus Homo*. In reaction from this fanciful formulation we are, however, too liable to discount the great truth which these fathers were seeking to express. That truth is the bearing which the redemptive work of Christ has upon the power and activity of Satan and upon the spiritual hosts of wickedness in the heavenlies (*cf.* Eph. 6:12). It is surely significant in this connection that the first promise of redemptive grace, the first beam of redemptive light that fell upon our fallen first parents, was in terms of the destruction of the tempter. And this same emphasis is embedded in the New Testament. As our Lord was approaching Calvary and as he had been reminded anew, by the request of the Greeks, of the worldwide significance of the work he was about to accomplish, it was then he took occasion to refer to the triumph over the archenemy and he said, "Now is the judgment of this world, now shall the prince of this world be cast out" (John 12:31). And for the apostle Paul the glory which radiated from the cross of Christ was a glory irradiated by the fact that "he spoiled the principalities and the powers and made a show of them openly, triumphing over them in it" (Col. 2:15). While we too often fail to reckon with the grim reality of death and are composed in its presence not because of faith but because of hardened insensitivity, it was not so in the fervor of New Testament faith. It was with depth of meaning that the writer of the epistle to the Hebrews wrote that Jesus partook of flesh and blood "that through death he might bring to nought him that had the power of death, that is the devil, and might deliver all them who through fear of death were all their lifetime subject to bondage" (Heb. 2:14-15). It was that triumph alone that released believers from the bondage of fear and inspired the confidence and composure of faith. But this triumph had relevance for them because their consciousness was one conditioned by the awareness of the role and activity of Satan, and confidence and composure entered their breasts because they knew that Christ's triumph terminated upon the sinister agent who had the power of death.

We thus see that redemption from sin cannot be adequately conceived or formulated except as it comprehends the victory which Christ secured once for all over him who is the god of this world, the prince of the power of the air, the spirit that now works in the children of disobedience. We must view sin and evil in its larger proportions as a kingdom that embraces the subtlety, craft, ingenuity, power, and unremitting activity of Satan and his legions — "the principalities, and the powers, the world-rulers of this darkness, the spiritual hosts of wickedness in the heavenlies" (Eph. 6:12). And it impossible to speak in terms of redemption from the power of sin except as there comes within the range of this redemptive accomplishment the destruction of the power of darkness. It is thus that we may entertain a more intelligent understanding of what Christ encountered when he said, "This is your hour and the power of darkness" (Luke 22:53) and of what the Lord of glory wrought when he cast out the prince of this world (John 12:31).

CHAPTER III

The Perfection of the Atonement

In Protestant polemics this feature of the atoning work of Christ has been oriented against the Romish tenet that the work of satisfaction accomplished by Christ does not relieve the faithful of the necessity of making satisfaction for sins which they have committed. According to Romish theology, all past sins both as respects their eternal and temporal punishment are blotted out in baptism and also the eternal punishment of the future sins of the faithful. But for the temporal punishment of post-baptismal sins the faithful must make satisfaction either in this life or in purgatory. In opposition to every such notion of human satisfaction Protestants rightly contend that the satisfaction of Christ is the only satisfaction for sin and is so perfect and final that it leaves no penal liability for any sin of the believer. It is true that in this life believers are chastised for their sins and such chastisement is corrective and sanctifying — "it yields the peaceable fruit of righteousness to them who are exercised thereby" (Heb. 12:11). And this chastisement is painful. But to approximate chastisement to satisfaction for sin is to impinge not only on the perfection of Christ's work but also upon the nature of Christ's satisfaction. "There is therefore now no condemnation to them who are in Christ Jesus" (Rom. 8:1). There must not be any abatement of the Protestant polemic against this perversion of the gospel of Christ. If we once allow the notion of human satisfaction to intrude itself in our construction of justification or sanctification then we have polluted the river the streams whereof make glad the city of God. And the gravest perversion that it entails is that it robs the Redeemer of the glory of his once-for-all accomplishment. He by himself purged our sins and sat down on the right hand of the majesty on high (*cf.* Heb. 1:3). The situation, however, in which we find ourselves in reference to debate upon the subject of the atonement requires us to take into account other ways in which the doctrine of the perfection of the atonement has been prejudiced and it is necessary for us to subsume under this caption other features of the finished work of Christ.

1. *The Historic Objectivity.* In the atonement something was accomplished once for all, without any participation or contribution on our part. A work was perfected which antedates any and every recognition or response on the part of those who are its beneficiaries. Any curtailing of this fact in the interest of what is supposed to be a more ethical interpretation or in the interest of interpreting the atonement in terms of the ethical effects it is calculated to produce in us is to eviscerate the truth of the atonement. The atonement is objective to us, performed independently of us, and the subjective effects that accrue from it presuppose its accomplishment. The subjective effects exerted in our understanding and will can follow only as we recognize by faith the meaning of the objective fact.

There is another implication of its historic objectivity that needs to be stressed. It is the strictly historical character of that which was accomplished. The atonement is not suprahistorical nor is it contemporary. It is indeed true that the person who atoned for sin is above history as regards his deity and eternal Sonship. As such he is eternal and transcends all the conditions and circumstances of time. He is with the

Father and Spirit the God of history. It is also true that as the incarnate Son exalted to the right hand of God he is in a true sense contemporary. He ever lives and as the living one who was dead but is alive again he is the ever-present and ever-active embodiment of the efficacy, virtue, and power accruing from the atonement. But the atonement was made in human nature and at a particular season in the past and finished calendar of events. Could anything point up the truth and significance of this more clearly than the word of the apostle, "When the fulness of the time was come, God sent forth his Son, made of a woman, made under the law, to redeem them that were under law" (Gal. 4:4-5)? Whether we interpret "the fulness of the time" as the full measure of the time appointed by God, the period that had to run its course before God sent forth his Son or as the time which consummates time and gives time its full complement, we must recognize the significance of time for that mission which is registered in and signalized by the incarnation of the Son of God. The incarnation occurred at a specific point marked by the arrival of the fullness of time; it did not occur before then and, though the incarnate state is abiding, the incarnation did not occur again. History with its fixed appointments and well-defined periods has significance in the drama of divine accomplishment. The historical conditioning and locating of events in time cannot be erased nor their significance underestimated. And what is true of the event of the incarnation is true also of the redemption wrought. Both are historically located and neither is suprahistorical or contemporary.

2. *The Finality.* In historical polemics this feature of the atonement has been urged against the Romish doctrine of the sacrifice of the mass. This polemic against Romish blasphemy is just as necessary today as it was in the Reformation period. The atonement is a completed work, never repeated and unrepeatable. In our modern context, however, it

is necessary to insist upon this tenet not only in opposition to Rome but also in opposition to a viewpoint prevalent within Protestant circles. This viewpoint is that the divine sin-bearing cannot be confined to the historical event of Jesus' sacrifice but must be regarded as eternal, that the work of atonement, incarnate in the passion of Jesus Christ, is eternal in the heavens in the very life of God, "an eternal work of atonement, supratemporal as the life of God is ... and going on as long as sins continue to be committed and there are sinners to be reconciled."[1]

It is indeed highly necessary to recognize the continued high priestly activity of Christ in heaven. It is necessary to remember that he eternally embodies in himself the efficacy that accrued from his sacrifice upon earth and that it is in virtue of such efficacy that he exercises his heavenly ministry as the great High Priest of our profession. It is on this ground that he intercedes on behalf of his people. And it is by reason of the sympathy derived from his earthly temptations that he can be touched with the feeling of our infirmities. This is just saying that the unity of Christ's priestly office and activity must be fully appreciated. But that we must not disrupt the unity of his priestly functions does not mean that we are at liberty to confuse the distinct actions and phases of his priestly office. We must distinguish between the offering of sacrifice and the subsequent activity of the high priest. What the New Testament stresses is the historical once-for-allness of the sacrifice that expiated guilt and reconciled to God (cf. Heb. 1:3; 9:12, 25-28). To fail to assess the finality of this once-for-allness is to misconceive what atonement really is. In the biblical construction atonement cannot be conceived of apart from the conditions under which it is wrought. Two conditions, at least, are indispensable, humiliation and obe-

1. D. M. Baillie: *op. cit.*, p. 194, n. 1.

dience, and these as mutually conditioning one another. It runs counter to the whole tenor of Scripture to transfer atonement to that realm where it would be impossible for us to believe that these conditions exist.

Furthermore, if we are thinking of the formula, "eternal atonement in the heart of God" we must again make distinctions. It is true that the atonement issued from, and was the provision of, eternal love in the heart of God. But to conceive of atonement as eternal is to confuse the eternal and the temporal. What the witness of Scripture bears out unmistakeably is the real significance for God of the temporal accomplishment. To this it refers atonement and it does so definitely and decisively. Our definition of atonement must be derived from the atonement of which Scripture speaks. And the atonement of which Scripture speaks is the vicarious obedience, expiation, propitiation, reconciliation, and redemption performed by the Lord of glory when, once for all, he purged our sins and sat down at the right hand of the majesty on high.

3. *The Uniqueness.* Horace Bushnell has given us what is probably the most eloquent exposition and defense of the idea that the sacrifice of Christ is but the supreme illustration and vindication of the principle of self-sacrifice which is operative in the breast of every loving and holy being as that being is confronted with sin and evil. "Love is a principle essentially vicarious in its own nature," he says, "identifying the subject with others, so as to suffer their adversities and pains, and taking on itself the burden of their evils."[2] "There is a Gethsemane hid in all love" (*ibid.* p. 47). "Holding such a view of vicarious sacrifice, we must find it belonging to the essential nature of all holy virtue. We are also required, of course, to go forward and show how it pertains to all other good beings, as truly as to Christ himself in the flesh — how

2. *The Vicarious Sacrifice* (New York, 1891), p. 42.

the eternal Father before Christ, and the Holy Spirit coming after, and the good angels both before and after, all alike have borne the burdens, struggled in the pains of their vicarious feeling for men; and then, at last, how Christianity comes to its issue, in begetting in us the same vicarious love that reigns in all the glorified and good minds of the heavenly kingdom; gathering us in after Christ our Master, as they have learned to bear his cross, and be with him in his passion" (ibid. p. 53).

To distinguish truth from error and to unravel the fallacies in these quotations would take us far beyond our limits. It is true that the sacrifice of Christ is the supreme revelation of the love of God. It is true that the life, sufferings, and death of Christ provide us with the supreme example of virtue. It is true that the afflictions of the church fill up that which is behind of the afflictions of Christ and that through these afflictions of believers the atoning work of Christ realizes its purpose. But to aver that we have part in that which constituted the vicarious sacrifice of Christ is an entirely different matter. It is indefensible and perverse to place upon the terms "vicarious" and "sacrifice" a diluted connotation that will reduce the "vicarious sacrifice" of Christ to a denomination that will rob it of the unique and distinctive character which the Scripture applies to it. Christ has indeed given us an example that we should follow his steps. But it is never proposed that this emulation on our part is to extend to the work of expiation, propitiation, reconciliation, and redemption which he accomplished. We need but define atonement in Scriptural terms to recognize that Christ alone made it.

And not only so. By what warrant or by what reasoning may we infer that what is constitutive of, or is exemplified in, the vicarious sacrifice of Christ is that which applies to all holy love as it contemplates sin and evil? It is only by fatal confusion of categories that any such inference can be made plausible. The Scripture representation is that the Son of

God incarnate and he alone, to the exclusion of the Father and Spirit in the realm of the divine, to the exclusion of angels and men in the created order, gave himself a sacrifice to redeem us to God by his blood. From whatever angle we look upon his sacrifice we find its uniqueness to be as inviolable as the uniqueness of his person, of his mission, and of his office. Who is God-man but he alone? Who is great high priest to offer such sacrifice but he alone? Who shed such vicarious blood but he alone? Who entered in once for all into the holy place, having obtained eternal redemption, but he alone? We may well quote the words of Hugh Martin. They are taken from his masterful polemic against the dictum of F. W. Robertson that "vicarious sacrifice is the law of being." With reference to this Martin says, "A very oracular announcement! It is needless to say that we meet it with a direct denial. Vicarious sacrifice is not only not the law of being, it is not a law at all. It is one solitary, matchless, Divine *transaction* — never to be repeated, never to be equalled, never to be approached. It was the splendid and unexpected device of Divine wisdom, which in its disclosure flooded the minds of angels with the knowledge of God. It was the free counsel of the good pleasure of God's will. It was the sovereign appointment of His grace and love. We are robbed of the sovereign love of God by the notion that vicarious sacrifice is the 'law of being'."[3]

4. *The Intrinsic Efficacy.* In the polemics of historical theology this aspect of the atonement has been urged against the Remonstrant doctrine that Christ did something which God graciously accepts in place of full satisfaction to justice. The statement of the Westminster Confession of Faith is admirably framed in contradistinction from the Remonstrant position. "The Lord Jesus, by His perfect obedience, and sacrifice of Himself, which He, through the eternal Spirit, once

3. Op. cit., pp. 241f.

offered up unto God, hath fully satisfied the justice of His Father; and purchased, not only reconciliation, but an everlasting inheritance in the kingdom of heaven, for all those whom the Father hath given unto Him" (VIII, v).

It is necessary to conceive and formulate aright the relation of the grace of God to the atoning work of Christ. It was by the grace of God that Christ was given on our behalf. It was by his own grace that he gave himself. It would be wholly false to conceive of the work of Christ as bringing inducements to bear upon the Father so that he is thereby constrained to be loving and gracious. "But God being rich in mercy, on account of his great love wherewith he loved us, and we being dead in trespasses, hath quickened us together with Christ" (Eph. 2:4-5; cf. I John 4:9). The atonement is the provision of the Father's love and grace. But there is equal need for remembering that the work wrought by Christ was in itself intrinsically adequate to meet all the exigencies created by our sin and all the demands of God's holiness and justice. Christ discharged the debt of sin. He bore our sins and purged them. He did not make a token payment which God accepts in place of the whole. Our debts are not canceled; they are liquidated. Christ procured redemption and therefore he secured it. He met in himself and swallowed up the full toll of divine condemnation and judgment against sin. He wrought righteousness which is the proper ground of complete justification and the title to everlasting life. Grace thus reigns through *righteousness* unto eternal life through Jesus Christ our Lord (cf. Rom. 5:19, 21). He expiated guilt and "by one offering he hath perfected for ever them that are sanctified" (Heb. 10:14). "Being made perfect he became the author (the cause) of eternal salvation to all them that obey him" (Heb. 5:9). In a word, Jesus met all the exigencies arising from our sin and he *procured* all the benefits that lead to, and are consummated in, the liberty of the glory of the children of God.

CHAPTER IV

The Extent of the Atonement

The question of the extent of the atonement is simply: for
whom did Christ make atonement? In even simpler language it is: for whom did Christ die? It might appear that the
Bible gives an unambiguous answer to the effect that Christ
died for all men. For we read: "All we like sheep have gone
astray; we have turned away every one to his own way; and
the Lord hath laid on him the iniquity of us all" (Isa. 53:6).
It would be easy to argue that the denotation of the "all" in
the last clause is just as extensive as the number of those
who have gone astray and have turned every one to his own
way. If so, the conclusion would be that the Lord laid on his
Son the iniquity of all men and that he was made an offering
for the sin of all. Again we read: "But we see Jesus, who was
made a little lower than the angels for the suffering of death,
crowned with glory and honour; that he by the grace of God
should taste death for every man" (Heb. 2:9). And it might be
said that John puts the question beyond all debate when he
says: "And he is the propitiation for our sins: and not for ours
only, but also for the whole world" (1 John 2:2).

We are not to think, however, that the quotation of a
few texts like these and several others that might be quoted
determines the question. From beginning to end the Bible
uses expressions that are universal in form but cannot be in-

terpreted as meaning all men distributively and inclusively. Such words as "world" and "all" and such expressions as "every one" and "all men" do not always in Scripture mean every member of the human race. For example, when Paul says with reference to the unbelief of Israel, "For if their trespass is the riches of the world ... how much more their fulness" (Rom. 11:12), are we to suppose that he meant that the trespass of Israel brought the riches of which he is speaking to every person who had been, is now, and ever will be in the world? Such an interpretation would make nonsense. The word "world" would then have to include Israel which is here contrasted with the world. And it is not true that every member of the human race was enriched by the fall of Israel. When Paul used the word "world" here he meant the Gentile world as contrasted with Israel. The context makes this abundantly plain. So we have an example of the word "world" used in a restricted sense and does not mean all men distributively. Again, when Paul says, "As through one trespass judgment came upon all men unto condemnation, even so through one righteous act judgment came upon all men unto justification of life" (Rom. 5:18), are we to suppose that justification came upon the whole human race, upon all men distributively and inclusively? This cannot be Paul's meaning. He is dealing with actual justification, the justification that is in Christ and unto eternal life (cf. vers. 1, 16, 17, 21). And we cannot believe that such justification passed upon every member of the human race unless we believe that all men will ultimately be saved, something contrary to Paul's teaching elsewhere and to the teaching of Scripture in general. Consequently, though Paul uses the expression "all men" in the first part of the verse in the sense of all men universally, yet he must be using the same expression in the second part of the verse in a much more restricted sense, namely, of all those who will be actually justified. To take another example, when Paul says that "all things were lawful" for him (1 Cor. 6:12; 10:23), he did not mean that every conceivable thing was lawful for him. It was not lawful for him to transgress the commandments of God. The "all things" of which he speaks are defined and limited by the context. Numerous other examples might be quoted and cited to show that expressions like these, though universalistic in form, frequently bear a restricted reference and do not mean every person of the human race.

So it will not do to quote a few texts from the Bible in which such words as "world" and "all" occur in connection with the death of Christ and forthwith conclude that the question is settled in favor of universal atonement.

We can readily show the fallacy of this procedure in connection with a text like Hebrews 2:9. What provides the denotation of the "every one" in the clause in question? Undoubtedly the context. Of whom is the writer speaking in the context? He is speaking of the many sons to be brought to glory (ver. 10), of the sanctified who with the sanctifier are all of one (ver. 11), of those who are called the brethren of Christ (ver. 12), and of the children which God had given to him (ver. 13). It is this that supplies us with the scope and reference of the "every one" for whom Christ tasted death. Christ did taste death for every son to be brought to glory and for all the children whom God had given to him. But there is not the slightest warrant in this text to extend the reference of the vicarious death of Christ beyond those who are most expressly referred to in the context. This texts shows how plausible off-hand quotation may be and yet how baseless is such an appeal in support of a doctrine of universal atonement.

In continuing the analysis of this doctrine, it is necessary to be clear what the question is not. The question is not whether many benefits short of justification and salvation accrue to men from the death of Christ. The unbelieving and reprobate in this world enjoy numerous benefits that flow from the fact that Christ died and rose again. The mediatorial dominion of Christ is universal. Christ is head over all things and is given all authority in heaven and in earth. It is within this mediatorial dominion that all the blessings which men enjoy are dispensed. But this dominion Christ exercises on the basis and as the reward of his finished work of redemption. "He humbled himself and became obedient unto death, even the death of the cross. Wherefore God also hath highly exalted him and given him the name that is above every name" (Phil. 2:8-9). Consequently, since all benefits and blessings are within the realm of Christ's dominion and since this dominion rests upon his finished work of atonement, the benefits innumerable which are enjoyed by all men indiscriminately are related to the death of Christ and may be said to accrue from it in one way or another. If they thus flow from the death of Christ they were intended thus to flow. It is proper, therefore, to say that the enjoyment of certain benefits, even by the non-elect and reprobate, falls within the design of the death of Christ. The denial of universal atonement does not carry with it the denial of any such relation that the benefits enjoyed by all men may sustain to Christ's death and finished work. The real question is something very different.

The question is: on whose behalf did Christ offer himself a sacrifice? On whose behalf did he propitiate the wrath of God? Whom did he reconcile to God in the body of his flesh through death? Whom did he redeem from the curse of the law, from the guilt and power of sin, from the enthralling power and bondage of Satan? In whose stead and on whose behalf was he obedient unto death, even the death of the cross? These are precisely the questions that have to be asked and frankly faced if the matter of the extent of the atonement is to be placed in proper focus. The question is not the relation of the death of Christ to the numerous blessings which those who finally perish may partake of in this life, however important this question is in itself and in its proper place. The question is precisely the reference of the death of Christ when this death is viewed as vicarious death, that is to say, as vicarious obedience, as substitutionary sacrifice, and expiation, as effective propitiation, reconciliation, and redemption. In a word, it is the strict and proper connotation of the expression "died for" that must be kept in mind. When Paul says that Christ "died for us" (1 Thess. 5:10) or that "Christ died for our sins" (1 Cor. 15:3), he does not have in mind some blessing that may accrue from the death of Christ but of which we may be deprived in due time and which may thus be forfeited. He is thinking of the stupendous truth that Christ loved him and gave himself up for him (Gal. 2:20), that Christ died in his room and stead, and that therefore we have redemption through the blood of Christ.

If we concentrate on the thought of redemption, we shall be able perhaps to sense more readily the impossibility of universalizing the atonement. What does redemption mean? It does not mean redeemability, that we are placed in a redeemable position. It means that Christ purchased and procured redemption. This is the triumphant note of the New Testament whenever it plays on the redemptive chord. Christ redeemed us to God by his blood (Rev. 5:9). He obtained eternal redemption (Heb. 9:12). "He gave himself for us in order that he might redeem us from all iniquity and purify to himself a people for his own possession, zealous of good works" (Titus 2:14). It is to beggar the concept of redemption as an effective securement of release by price and by power to construe it as anything less than the effectual accomplishment which secures the salvation of those who are its objects. Christ did not come to put men in a redeemable position but to reedem to himself a people. We have the same result when we properly analyse the meaning of expiation, propitiation, and reconciliation. Christ did not come to make sins expiable. He came to expiate sins — "when he made purification of sins, he sat down on the right hand of the majesty on high" (Heb. 1:3). Christ did not come to make God reconcilable. He reconciled us to God by his own blood.

The very nature of Christ's mission and accomplishment is involved in this question. Did Christ come to make the salvation of all men possible, to remove obstacles that stood in the way of salvation, and merely to make provision for salvation? Or did he come to save his people? Did he come to put all men in a salvable state? Or did he come to secure the salvation of all those who are ordained to eternal life? Did he come to make men redeemable? Or did he come effectually and infallibly to redeem? The doctrine of the atonement must be radically revised if, as atonement, it applies to those who finally perish as well as to those who are the heirs of eternal life. In that event we should have to dilute the grand categories in terms of which the Scripture defines the atonement and deprive them of their most precious import and glory. This we cannot do. The saving efficacy of expiation, propitiation, reconciliation, and redemption is too deeply embedded in these concepts, and we dare not eliminate this efficacy. We do well to ponder the words of our Lord himself: "I have come down from heaven, not to do my own will but the will of him who sent me. And this is the will of him who sent me, that of everything which he hath given to me I should lose nothing, but should raise it up in the last day" (John 6:38-39). Security inheres in Christ's redemptive accomplishment. And this means that, in respect of the persons contemplated, design and accomplishment and final realization have all the same extent.

This doctrine has been called the doctrine of limited atonement. This may or may not be a good or fair denomination. But it is not the term used that is important; it is that which it denotes. It is very easy to raise prejudice against a doctrine by attaching to it an opprobrious and misunderstood epithet. Whether the expression "limited atonement" is good or not we must reckon with the fact that unless we believe in the final restoration of all men we cannot have an unlimited atonement. If we universalize the extent we limit the efficacy. If some of those for whom atonement was made and redemption wrought perish eternally, then the atonement is not itself efficacious. It is this alternative that the proponents of universal atonement must face. They have a "limited" atonement and limited in respect of that which impinges upon its essential character. We shall have none of it. The doctrine of "limited atonement" which we maintain is the doctrine which limits the atonement to those who are heirs of eternal life, to the elect. That limitation insures its efficacy and conserves its essential character as efficient and effective redemption.

It is frequently objected that this doctrine is inconsistent with the full and free offer of Christ in the gospel. This is grave misunderstanding and misrepresentation. The truth really is that it is only on the basis of such a doctrine that we can have a free and full offer of Christ to lost men. What is offered to men in the gospel? It is not the possibility of salvation, not simply the opportunity of salvation. What is offered is salvation. To be more specific, it is Christ himself in all the glory of his person and in all the perfection of his finished work who is offered. And he is offered as the one who made expiation for sin and wrought redemption. But he could not be offered in this capacity or character if he had not secured salvation and accomplished redemption. He could not be offered as Savior and as the one who embodies in himself salvation full and free if he had simply made the salvation of all men possible or merely had made provision for the salvation of all. It is the very doctrine that Christ procured and secured redemption that invests the free offer of the gospel with richness and power. It is that doctrine alone that allows for a presentation of Christ that will be worthy of the glory of his accomplishment and of his person. It is because Christ procured and secured redemption that he is an all-sufficient and suitable Savior. It is as such he is offered, and the faith that this offer demands is the faith of self-commitment to him as the one who is the eternal embodiment of the efficacy accruing from obedience completed and redemption secured.

It is proper, however, that the inquirer should ask the question: is there not also more direct evidence provided by the Scripture to show the definite or limited extent of the atonement? There are indeed many biblical arguments. We shall content ourselves with setting forth two of these, not because there are only two but because these are examples of the evidence which the Scripture itself provides to show the necessity of this doctrine.

1. The first is drawn from Romans 8:31-39. There is no question but that on two occasions in this passage explicit reference is made to the death of Christ — "he that spared not his own Son but delivered him up for us all" (ver. 32) and "Christ Jesus is the one who died, yea rather is raised up" (ver. 34). Hence any indication given in this passage respecting extent would be pertinent to the question of the extent of the atonement.

In verse 31 Paul asks the question: "What shall we then say to these things? If God is for us, who is against us?" We are compelled to ask the question: of whom is Paul speaking? In other words, what is the denotation of the expressions "for us" and "against us"? The answer is that the denotation cannot be other than that provided by the preceding context, namely, those spoken of in verses 28-30. It would be impossible to universalize the denotation of verse 31 if we are to think biblically, and it would be exegetically monstrous to break the continuity of Paul's thought and extend the reference of verse 31 beyond the scope of those spoken of in verse 30. This means therefore that the denotation in view in the words "for us" and "against us" in verse 31 is restricted, and restricted in terms of verse 30.

When we proceed to verse 32 we find that Paul again uses this expression "for us" and adds the word "all" — "he that spared not his own Son but delivered him up *for us all.*" Here he is dealing expressly with those on whose behalf the Father delivered up the Son. And the question is: what is the scope of the expression, "for us all"? It would be absurd to insist that the presence of the word "all" has the effect of universalizing the scope. The "all" is not broader than the "us." Paul is saying that the action of the Father in view was on behalf of "all of us" and the question is simply the scope of the "us." The only proper answer to this question is that the "us" in view in verse 32 is the "us" in view in verse 31. It would be doing violence to the most elementary rules of interpretation to suppose that at verse 32 Paul had broadened the scope of those to whom he is speaking and included many more than he included in the protestation of verse 31. In fact Paul is continuing his protestation and saying that not only is God for us but will also freely give us all things. And the guarantee of this resides in the fact that the Father gave up his Son on our behalf. Lest there should be any doubt as to the restricted denotation of the words, "for us all" in verse 32, it is well to be reminded that the giving up of the Son is correlative with the free bestowal of all good gifts. We may not extend the scope of the sacrifice of the Son beyond the scope of all the other free gifts — every one on whose behalf the Father delivered up the Son becomes the beneficiary of all other gifts of grace. To put it briefly, those contemplated in the sacrifice of Christ are also the partakers of the other gifts of saving grace — "how shall he not with him also freely give us all things?"

When we proceed to verse 33 the restrictive scope becomes unquestionably patent. For Paul says: "who will bring a charge against the elect of God? God is the one who justifies: who is he who condemns?" The thought moves strictly within the orbit defined by election and justification, and the reference to election and justification harks back to verses 28-30 where predestination and justification are shown to be coextensive.

At verse 34 Paul again refers to the death of Christ. He does so in a way that is significant for our present interest in two respects. His appeal to the death of Christ is co-ordinated with the fact that it is God who justifies. And he does this for the purpose of vindicating the elect of God against any charge that might be brought against them and to support his challenge, "who shall lay a charge against the elect of God?" It is the elect and the justified that Paul has in mind here in his appeal to the death of Christ and there is no reason for going outside the denotation provided by election and justification when we seek to discover the extent of Christ's sacrificial death. The second respect in which his reference here to the death of Christ is significant is that he appeals to the death of Christ in the context of its sequel in the resurrection the session at the right hand of God, and the intercession on our behalf. Again Paul uses this expression "for us" and he uses it now in connection with intercession — "who also makes intercession for us." Two observations bear directly upon our question. First, the expression "for us" in this case must be given the restricted denotation which we found already in verse 31. It is impossible to universalize it not only because of the restrictive scope of the whole context but also because of the very nature of intercession as availing and efficacious. Second, because of the way in which the death, resurrection, and intercession of Christ are co-ordinated in this passage, it would be quite unwarranted to give to the death of Christ a more inclusive reference than is given to his intercession. When Paul says here, "it is Christ that died," he of course means that "Christ died for us," just as in verse 32 he says that the Father "delivered him up for us all." We cannot give wider scope to the "for us" implied in the clause, "it is Christ that died" than we can give to the "for us" expressly stated in the clause, "who also makes intercession for us." Hence we see that we are led into impossible suppositions if we try to universalize the denotation of those referred to in these passages.

Finally, we have the most cogent consideration of all. "Who shall separate us from the love of Christ? ... For I am persuaded that neither death nor life nor angels nor principalities nor things present nor things to come nor powers nor height nor depth nor any other creature will be able to separate us from the love of God which is in Christ Jesus our Lord" (Rom. 8:35-39). Paul is here affirming in the most emphatic way, in one of the most rhetorical conclusions of his epistles, the security of those of whom he has been speaking. The guarantee of this security is the love of God which is in Christ Jesus. And the love of God here spoken of is undoubtedly the love of God towards those who are embraced in it. Now the inevitable inference is that this love from which it is impossible to be separated and which guarantees the bliss of those who are embraced in it is the same love that must be alluded to earlier in the passage when Paul says, "He that spared not his own Son but delivered him up for us all, how shall he not with him also freely give us all things?" (ver. 32). It is surely the same love, called in verse 39 "the love of God which is in Christ Jesus," that constrained the Father to deliver up his own Son. This means that the love implied in verse 32, the love of giving the Son, cannot be given a wider reference than the love which, according to verses 35-39, insures the eternal security of those who are its objects. If not all men enjoy this security, how can that which is the source of this security and the guarantee of its possession embrace those who enjoy no such security? We see, therefore, that the security of which Paul here speaks is a security restricted to those who are the objects of the love which was exhibited on Calvary's accursed tree, and therefore the love exhibited on Calvary is itself a distinguishing love and not a love that is indiscriminately universal. It is a love that insures the eternal security of those who are its objects and Calvary itself is that which secures for them the justifying righteousness through which eternal life reigns. And this is just saying that the atonement which Calvary accomplished is not itself universal.

2. The second biblical argument that we may adduce in support of the doctrine of definite atonement is that drawn from the fact that those for whom Christ died have themselves also died in Christ. In the New Testament the more common way of representing the relation of believers to the death of Christ is to say that Christ died for them. But there is also the strand of teaching to the effect that they died in Christ (cf. Rom. 6:3-11; 2 Cor. 5:14-15; Eph. 2:4-7; Col. 3:3). There can be no doubt respecting the proposition that all for whom Christ died also died in Christ. For Paul says explicitly, "one died for all: therefore all died" (2 Cor. 5:14) — there is denotative equation.

The significant feature of this teaching of the apostle for our present interest is, however, that all who died in Christ rose again with him. This also Paul states explicitly. "But if we died with Christ, we believe that we shall also live with him, knowing that Christ being raised from the dead dieth no more, death hath no more dominion over him" (Rom. 6:8-9). Just as Christ died and rose again, so all who died in him rose again in him. And when we ask the question what this rising again in Christ involves, Paul leaves us in no doubt — it is a rising again to newness of life. "Therefore we were buried with him through baptism into death, in order that as Christ was raised from the dead through the glory of the Father, even so we should walk in newness of life. For if we have been planted together in the likeness of his death, we shall be also in the likeness of the resurrection" (Rom. 6:4-5). "For the love of Christ constraineth us, because we thus judge, that one died for all, therefore all died: and he died for all in order that those who live should no longer live to themselves but to him who died for them and rose again" (2 Cor. 5:14-15). "For ye died, and your life is hid with Christ in God" (Col. 3:3).

We have, therefore, the following sequence of propositions, established by the explicit utterances of the apostle. All for whom Christ died also died in Christ. All who died in Christ rose again with Christ. This rising again with Christ is a rising to newness of life after the likeness of Christ's resurrection. To die with Christ is, therefore, to die to sin and to rise with him to the life of new obedience, to live not to ourselves but to him who died for us and rose again. The inference is inevitable that those for whom Christ died are those and those only who die to sin and live to righteousness. Now it is a plain fact that not all die to sin and live in newness of life. Hence we cannot say that all men distributively died with Christ. And neither can we say that Christ died for all men, for the simple reason that all for whom Christ died also died in Christ. If we cannot say that Christ died for all men, neither can we say that the atonement is universal — it is the death of Christ for men that specifically constitutes the atonement. The conclusion is apparent — the death of Christ in its specific character as atonement was for those and those only who are in due time the partakers of that new life of which Christ's resurrection is the pledge and pattern. This is another reminder that the death and resurrection of Christ are inseparable. Those for whom Christ died are those for whom he rose again and his heavenly saving activity is of equal extent with his once-for-all redemptive accomplishments.

In concluding our discussion of the extent of the atonement it may be well to reflect upon one or two passages which have frequently been appealed to as settling the debate in favor of universal atonement. Second Corinthians 5:14-15 is one of these. On two occasions in this text Paul says that Christ "died for all." But that this expression is not to be understood as distributively universal can be shown by the terms of the passage itself when interpreted in the light of Paul's teaching. We have found already that according to Paul's teaching all for whom Christ died also died in Christ. He states that truth emphatically here — "one died for all: therefore all died." But elsewhere he makes perfectly plain that those who died in Christ rise again with him (Rom. 6:8). Although this latter truth is not stated in so many words in this passage, it is surely implied in the words, "he (Christ) died for all in order that those who live should not henceforth live unto themselves but unto him who died for them and rose again." If we were to suppose that the expression, "those who live" is restrictive and does not have the same extent as the "all" for whom Christ died, this would bring us into conflict with the explicit affirmations of Paul in Romans 6:5, 8 to the effect that those who have been planted in the likeness of Christ's death will be also in the likeness of his resurrection and that those who died with him will also live with him. The analogy of Paul's teaching in Romans 6:4-8 must be applied to 2 Corinthians 5:14-15. Hence those referred to as "those who live" must have the same extent as those embraced in the preceding clause, "he died for all." And since "those who live" do not embrace the whole human race, neither can the "all" referred to in the clause, "he died for all" embrace the entire human family. Corroboration is derived from the concluding words of verse 15, "but to him who died for them and rose again." Here again the death and resurrection of Christ are conjoined and the analogy of Paul's teaching in similar contexts is to the effect that those who are the beneficiaries of Christ's death are also of his resurrection and therefore of his resurrection life. So when Paul says here, "died for them and rose again" the implication is that those for whom he died are those for whom he rose, and those for whom he rose are those who live in newness of life. In terms of Paul's teaching then and, specifically, in terms of the import of this passage we cannot interpret the "for all" of 2 Corinthians 5:14-15 as distributively universal. So far from lending support to the doctrine of universal atonement this text does the opposite.

Perhaps no text in Scripture presents more plausible support to the doctrine of universal atonement than 1 John 2:2: "And he is the propitiation for our sins, and not for ours only but also for the whole world." The extension of the propitiation to "the whole world" would appear to allow for no other construction than that the propitiation for sins embraces the sins of the whole world. It must be said that the language John uses here would fit in perfectly with the doctrine of universal atonement if Scripture elsewhere demonstrated that to be the biblical doctrine. And it must also be said that this expression of itself would not offer any proof of or support to a doctrine of limited atonement. The question however is: does this text prove that the atonement is universal? In other words, is the case such that canons of interpretation are violated if we interpret it in a way that is compatible with the doctrine of limited atonement? Since there are so many biblical reasons for the doctrine of a limited extent of the atonement we are required to ask this question, and when we seek to answer it we can find several reasons why John should have said "for the whole world" without in the least implying that his intent was to teach what the proponents of universal atonement allege. There is good reason why John should have said "for the whole world" quite apart from the assumption of universal atonement.

1. It was necessary for John to set forth the *scope* of Jesus' propitiation — it was not limited in its virtue and efficacy to the immediate circle of disciples who had actually seen and heard and handled the Lord in the days of his sojourn upon earth (*cf.* 1 John 1:1-3), nor to the circle of believers who came directly under the influence of the apostolic witness (*cf.* 1 John 1:3-4). The propitiation which Jesus himself is extends in its virtue, efficacy, and intent to all in every nation who through the apostolic witness came to have fellowship with the Father and the Son (*cf.* 1 John 1:5-7). Every nation and kindred and people and tongue is in this sense embraced in the propitiation. It was highly necessary that John, like the other writers of the New Testament and like the Lord himself, should stress the ethnic universalism of the gospel and therefore of Jesus' propitiation as the central message of that gospel. John needed to say, in order to proclaim this universalism of gospel grace, "not for ours only but also for the whole world."

2. It was necessary for John to emphasize the *exclusiveness* of Jesus as the propitiation. It is this propitiation that is the one and only specific for the remission of sin. John in the context was underscoring the gravity of sin and the necessity of avoiding the snare of complacency with reference to it. But in that connection it was imperative for him to remind believers that there is no other laver for sin than Jesus' propitiation — there is no other sacrifice for sin. The utmost bounds of human need and the utmost bounds of divine grace know no other propitiation — it is for the whole world.

3. It was necessary for John to remind his readers of the *perpetuity* of Jesus' propitiation. It is this propitiation that endures as such through all ages — its efficacy is never di-

minished, it never loses any of its virtue. And not only is it everlasting in its efficacy but it is the perpetual propitiatory for the ever-recurring and ever-continuing sins of believers — they do not plead another propitiation for the sins they continue to commit any more than do they appeal to another advocate with the Father for the liabilities which their continuing sins entail.

Hence the scope, the exclusiveness, and the perpetuity of the propitiation provided sufficient reason for John to say, "not for ours only but also for the whole world." And we need not suppose that John was here enunciating a doctrine of propitiation that is distributively universal in its extent. If it is not necessary to find a doctrine of universal atonement in 1 John 2:2, then this text does not establish universal atonement and the meaning and intent can be harmonized with what we find to be the doctrine required by other biblical considerations.

It is worthy of note that John in this text speaks of Jesus as the propitiation — "and he is the propitiation for our sins." It is highly probable that this form of statement points to "Jesus Christ the righteous" as not only the one who made propitiation once for all by his sacrifice on the cross but as the one who is the abiding embodiment of the propitiatory virtue accruing from his once-for-all accomplishment and also as the one who offers to those who trust in him an ever-availing propitiatory. This threefold aspect from which propitiation may be viewed is of the deepest significance for the consolation of the people of God as they consider what, above all else, is the liability created by their sin, namely, the displeasure of God. Christ is the abiding propitiatory so that they may draw near in full assurance of faith knowing that the propitiation which Christ rendered and the propitiatory which he ever continues to be constitute the guarantee that they will be saved from the wrath which their sins deserve.

It is this complex of thought that makes it difficult for us to place even this text in the framework of universal propitiation. There is here, as in so many other instances, a certain concatenation by which the efficacy that accrues from the atonement is conjoined with the atonement. And as we take into account the thought of the preceding verse that Jesus Christ is our advocate with the Father, it is necessary to regard the advocacy which Jesus renders and the propitiation that he is as complementary. It is because Jesus made propitiation and is the abiding propitiatory that he is the advocate with the Father. If we give to the propitiation an extent far beyond that of his advocacy we inject something which is hardly compatible with this complementation.

We can readily see, therefore, that although universal terms are sometimes used in connection with the atonement these terms cannot be appealed to as establishing the doctrine of universal atonement. In some cases, as we have found, it can be shown that all-inclusive universalism is excluded by the considerations of the immediate context. In other cases there are adequate reasons why universal terms should be used without the implication of distributively universal extent. Hence no conclusive support for the doctrine of universal atonement can be derived from universalistic expressions. The question must be determined on the basis of other evidence. This evidence we have tried to present. It is easy for the proponents of universal atonement to make offhand appeal to a few texts. But this method is not worthy of the serious student of Scripture. It is necessary for us to discover what redemption or atonement really means. And when we examine the Scripture we find that the glory of the cross of Christ is bound up with the effectiveness of its accomplishment. Christ redeemed us to God by his blood, he gave himself a ransom that he might deliver us from all iniquity. The atonement is efficacious substitution.

CHAPTER V

Conclusion

There is only one source from which we can derive a proper conception of Christ's atoning work. That source is the Bible. There is only one norm by which our interpretations and formulations are to be tested. That norm is the Bible. The temptation ever lurks near us to prove unfaithful to this one and only criterion. No temptation is more subtle and plausible than the tendency to construe the atonement in terms of our human experience and thus to make our experience the norm. It does not always appear in its undisguised form. But it is the same tendency that underlies the attempt to place upon the work of Christ an interpretation which brings it into closer approximation to human experience and accomplishment, the attempt to accommodate our interpretation and application of our Lord's suffering and obedience unto death to the measure or, at least, to the analogy of our experience. There are two directions in which we can do this. We can heighten the significance of our experience and doing to the measure of our Lord's or we can lower the significance of our Lord's experience and doing to the measure of ours. The bias and the final result are the same. We drag down the meaning of Christ's atoning work and we evacuate it of its unique and distinctive glory. This is wickedness of the deepest dye. What human experience can reproduce that which the Lord of glory, the Son of God incarnate, alone endured and accomplished?

It is true we bear the punishment of our sins and we may know something of the bitterness. We are subject to the wrath of God, and the sting of unremitted guilt can reflect the awful severity of divine displeasure. Our sins have separated us from God and we can know the dismal emptiness of being without God and without hope in the world. There is still more we can know of the bitterness of sin and death. The lost in perdition will everlastingly bear the unrelieved and unmitigated judgment due to their sins; they will eternally suffer in the exaction of the demands of justice. But there was only one, and there will not need to be another, who bore the full weight of the divine judgment upon sin and bore it so as to end it. The lost will eternally suffer in the satisfaction of justice. But they will never satisfy it. Christ *satisfied* justice. "The Lord hath laid on him the iniquity of us all" (Isa. 53:6). He was made sin and he was made a curse. He bore our iniquities. He bore the unrelieved and unmitigated damnation of sin, and he finished it. That is the spectacle that confronts us in Gethsemane and on Calvary. This is the explanation of Gethsemane with its bloody sweat and agonizing cry, "O my Father, if it be possible, let this cup pass from me" (Matt. 26:39). And this is the explanation of the most mysterious utterance that ever ascended from earth to heaven, "My God, my God, why hast thou forsaken me?" Perish the thought that "there is a Gethsemane hid in all love!" And perish the presumption that dares to speak of our Gethsemanes and Calvaries! It is trifling with the most solemn spectacle in all history, a spectacle unparalleled, unique, unrepeated, and unrepeatable. To approximate this spectacle to the analogy of our human experience is to disclose a state of mind and feeling insensitive to the alphabet of Christianity. Here we are the spectators of a wonder the praise and glory of which eternity will not exhaust. It is the Lord of glory, the Son of God incarnate, the God-man, drinking the cup given him by the eternal Father, the cup of woe and of indescribable agony. We almost hesitate to say so. But it must be said. It is God in our nature forsaken of God. The cry from the accursed tree evinces nothing less than the abandonment that is the wages of sin. And it was abandonment endured vicariously because he bore our sins in his own body on the tree. There is no analogy. He himself bore our sins and of the people there was none with him. There is no reproduction or parallel in the experience of archangels or of the greatest saints. The faintest parallel would crush the holiest of men and the mightiest of the angelic host.

Who will say that the vicarious endurance of the unrelieved and unmitigated judgment of God upon sin impairs the initiative and character of eternal love? It is the spectacle of Gethsemane and Calvary, thus interpreted, that opens to us the folds of unspeakable love. The Father did not spare his own Son. He spared nothing that the dictates of unrelenting rectitude demanded. And it is the undercurrent of the Son's acquiescence that we hear when he says, "Nevertheless not my will, but thine, be done" (Luke 22:42). But why? It was in order that eternal and invincible love might find the full realization of its urge and purpose in redemption by price and by power. Of Calvary the spirit is eternal love and the basis eternal justice. It is the same love manifested in the mystery of Gethsemane's agony and of Calvary's accursed tree that wraps eternal security around the people of God. "He that spared not his own Son, but delivered him up for us all, how shall he not with him also freely give us all things?" (Rom. 8:32). "Who shall separate us from the love of Christ? shall tribulation, or distress, or persecution, or famine, or nakedness, or peril, or sword?" (Rom. 8:35). "For I am persuaded that neither death nor life nor angels nor principalities nor things present nor things to come nor powers nor height nor depth nor any other creature will be able to separate us from the love of God which is in Christ Jesus our Lord" (Rom. 8:38-39). That is the security which a perfect atonement secures and it is the perfection of the atonement that secures it.

PART II

Redemption Applied

CHAPTER I

The Order of Application

The provision which God has made in his providence for the sustenance and comfort of man and beast is not sparing or niggardly. He has made the earth to teem with good things to satisfy the needs of man and beast and to meet their varied tastes and appetites. Psalm 104 is the inspired lyric of praise and admiration. "These wait all upon thee; that thou mayest give them their meat in due season ... thou openest thine hand, they are filled with good" (vers. 27-28). "Wine that maketh glad the heart of man, oil to make his face to shine, and bread which strengtheneth man's heart" (ver. 15). And the psalmist exclaims: "O Lord, how manifold are thy works! in wisdom hast thou made them all: the earth is full of thy riches" (ver. 24).

The provision which God has made for the salvation of men is even more strikingly manifold. For this provision has in view the manifoldness of man's need and exhibits the overflowing abundance of God's goodness, wisdom, grace, and love. This superabundance appears in the eternal counsel of God respecting salvation; it appears in the historic accomplishment of redemption by the work of Christ once for all; and it appears in the application of redemption continuously and progressively till it reaches its consummation in the liberty of the glory of the children of God.

When we think of the application of redemption we must not think of it as one simple and indivisible act. It comprises a series of acts and processes. To mention some, we have calling, regeneration, justification, adoption, sanctification, glorification. These are all distinct, and not one of these can be defined in terms of the other. Each has its own distinct meaning, function, and purpose in the action and grace of God.

God is not the author of confusion and therefore he is the author of order. There are good and conclusive reasons for thinking that the various actions of the application of redemption, some of which have been mentioned, take place in a certain order, and that order has been established by divine appointment, wisdom, and grace. It is quite apparent to every one that it would be impossible to start off with glorification, for glorification is at the far end of the process as its completion and consummation, and it is scarcely less apparent that regeneration would have to precede sanctification. A man must surely be born again before he can be progressively sanctified. Regeneration is the inception of being made holy and sanctification is the continuance. Hence it requires no more than the most elementary knowledge of these various terms to see that we cannot turn them around and mix them up in any way we please. But we may also look at a few passages of Scripture to show that there is clearly implied an order or arrangement in the various steps of the application of redemption.

If we take, first of all, such well-known texts as John 3:3, 5, our Lord told Nicodemus that except a man be born from above he cannot see the kingdom of God and except a man be born of water and of the Spirit he cannot enter into the kingdom of God. Obviously, seeing and entering into the kingdom of God belong to the application of redemption, and our Lord indicates that apart from the new birth, regeneration, there cannot be this seeing or entering into the kingdom of God. It follows that regeneration is prior and it would plainly be impossible to reverse the order and say that a man is regenerated by seeing or entering into the kingdom of God. No, a man enters the kingdom of God by regeneration. As Jesus says again (John 3:6), "that which is born of the Spirit is spirit."

We may also examine a closely related text, 1 John 3:9: "Every one who is born of God does not do sin, because his seed remains in him; and he cannot sin, because he is born of God." John is dealing here, no doubt, with deliverance from the reigning power of sin. Such deliverance is part of the application of redemption. But the text demonstrates that the reason why a person is delivered from the reigning power of sin is that he is born of God, and the reason he continues in this freedom from the ruling and directing power of sin is that the seed of God abides in him. Here we have clearly the order of causation and explanation. The new birth causes and explains the state of freedom from the domination of sin and is therefore prior to such freedom. The regenerated person does not commit the sin which is unto death (1 John 5:16) and the reason is that he is born of God and God's seed is always in him to keep him from that grievous and irreparable sin.

Still further, let us look at John 1:12. We may focus our attention on two subjects with which this text deals, namely, the reception of Christ and the bestowment of authority to become the sons of God. We may properly call them faith and adoption. The text says distinctly that "as many as received him, to them gave he authority to become children of God." The bestowment of this authority, which we may for our present purposes equate with adoption, presupposes the reception of Christ, namely, faith in his name. This is to the effect of saying that adoption presupposes faith, and therefore faith is prior to adoption. So we should have to follow the order, faith and adoption.

Finally, we may glance at one passage in Paul, Ephesians 1:13: "In whom ye also, having heard the word of truth, the gospel of your salvation, in whom also having believed ye were sealed with the Holy Spirit of promise." The sealing with the Holy Spirit is that which follows upon the hearing of the word of truth and believing. Hearing and believing are therefore prior in order and cannot be made to follow the sealing of the Spirit.

These few texts have been appealed to simply for the purpose of showing that there is order which must be maintained and cannot be reversed without violating the plain import of these texts. These texts prove the fact of order and show that it is not empty logic to affirm divine order in the application of redemption. There is a divine logic in this matter and the order which we insist upon should be nothing more or less than what the Scriptures disclose to be the divine arrangement.

These texts, however, have not brought us very far in discovering what the order of arrangement is in connection with a good many of the actions which are comprised in the application of redemption. They have established a few things, indeed, but only a few. When we give a fuller enumeration of the several steps or aspects — calling, regeneration, conversion, faith, repentance, justification, adoption, sanctification, perseverance, glorification — we can see that several questions remain undetermined. Which is prior, calling or justification? Is faith prior to justification or *vice versa*? Does regeneration come before calling?

There is one passage of Scripture which affords us a great deal of light on this question. It is Romans 8:30: "Moreover whom he did predestinate, them he also called; and whom he called, them he also justified: and whom he justified, them he also glorified." Here we have three acts of the application of redemption — calling, justification, and glorification. They appear in this text in that order. And the question arises: is this order intended to be the order of application and occurrence? Or is the order in the text simply one of convenience so that Paul could just as well have adopted another order?

One thing must be said by way of preface; it is that even if the order had been different, justification first and calling second, the main thought of the passage would not be disturbed. The main thought is the invariable conjunction and sequence of these divine acts and their indissoluble connection with God's eternal purpose of foreknowledge and predestination. For here we have a chain of unbreakable links beginning with foreknowledge and ending with glorification.

But there are overwhelming reasons for thinking that the order Paul follows in verse 30 — calling, justification, glorification — is the order of sequence according to the divine arrangement. These reasons are not far to seek. There are so many intimations of order in this passage as a whole that we cannot but conclude that order of logical sequence is intended throughout.

1. In verse 28 there is the intimation of order in the expression, "called according to purpose." This means that purpose provides the pattern or plan according to which calling takes place. Therefore the purpose is prior to the calling, and, in this case, of course, eternally prior. The purpose is none other than that which is unfolded in verse 29 as consisting in foreknowledge and predestination. Hence we have a clear indication of order in verse 28.

2. We have the same in verse 29. It is not our interest now to expound the meaning of the word "foreknow" nor its relation to the word "predestinate." All that is necessary to note now is that there is progression of thought from foreknowledge to predestination. Here again we have an indication of order which will not allow us to reverse the elements involved.

3. In verses 29 and 30 we have a chain of events which find their spring in foreknowledge and their terminus in glorification. We cannot possibly reverse these two. There is not only priority and posteriority but a particular kind of such order, namely, foreknowledge as the ultimate fount and glorification as the ultimate end.

4. The same applies to both foreknowledge and predestination in reference to the three acts mentioned in verse 30. Foreknowledge and predestination are prior to calling, justification, and glorification, and eternally prior at that. Reversal is inconceivable.

5. Even within the acts mentioned in verse 30, acts which fall within the sphere of the application of redemption and which are therefore temporal as distinguished from those of God's eternal counsel mentioned in verse 29, we are bound to discover an order of priority. Glorification could not be prior to calling and justification; it must be posterior to both. Hence, whatever may be true as regards the order of calling and justification in relation to each other, glorification must be after both. The only question that remains, therefore, is whether calling is prior to justification or the reverse.

We shall have to conclude that, since there are so many indications of intended order in this passage as a whole, the order which Paul follows in reference to calling and justification must be intended as the order of logical arrangement and progression. It would violate every relevant consideration to think otherwise. Consequently we must infer that Romans 8:30 provides us with a broad outline of the order in the application of redemption and that that order is: calling, justification, glorification. So we have the answer to one question, which has not so far been determined, namely, that calling precedes justification in the order of the application of redemption. And we might not have thought so if we were to rely upon our own logical reasonings.

The next question we may discuss is the relation of faith to justification. There is difference of judgment on this question among orthodox theologians, some holding that justification is prior, others the reverse. It must be understood that what we are dealing with now is not at all God's eternal decree to justify. That certainly is prior to faith, and, if we were to call that "eternal justification" (a misuse of terms), then such would be prior to faith just as God's purpose is always prior to every phase of the application of redemption. Furthermore, if we use the term justification as the virtual synonym of reconciliation (as it may be in Romans 5:9), then again such justification is prior to faith just as the accomplishment of redemption is always prior to the application of it. But we are not now dealing with the eternal decree to justify nor with the basis of justification in the work once for all accomplished by Christ but with actual justification, which falls within the orbit of the application of redemption. With reference to such justification the Scripture undoubtedly states that we are justified by faith, from faith, through faith, and upon faith (see Rom. 1:17; 3:22, 26, 28, 30; 5:1; Gal. 2:16; 3:24; Phil. 3:9). It would surely seem impossible to avoid the conclusion that justification is upon the event of faith or through the instrumentality of faith. God justifies the ungodly who believe in Jesus, in a word, believers. And that is simply to say that faith is presupposed in justification, is the precondition of justification, not because we are justified on the ground of faith or for the reason that we are justified because of faith but only for the reason that faith is God's appointed instrument through which he dispenses this grace.

There is another reason why we should believe that faith is prior to justification. We found already that calling is prior to justification. And faith is connected with calling. It does not constitute calling. But it is the inevitable response of our heart and mind and will to the divine call. In this matter call and response coincide. For that reason we should expect that since calling is prior to justification so is faith. This inference is confirmed by the express statement that we are justified by faith.

We are now in a position to give the following, slightly enlarged outline of the order in the application of redemption — calling, faith, justification, glorification.

If we think in Scriptural terms it is not difficult to insert another step. It is that of regeneration. It, in turn, must be prior to faith. Much controversy turns on this question and into all the angles of that controversy we need not enter. Still further, it will not be possible in this chapter to give all the evidence establishing the priority of regeneration. A good deal of that evidence will be presented later. Suffice it at present to be reminded that as sinners we are dead in trespasses and sins. Faith is a whole-souled act of loving trust and self-commitment. Of that we are incapable until renewed by the Holy Spirit. It was to this our Lord testified when he said that no one could come unto him except it were given unto him of the Father and except the Father draw him (John 6:44, 65). And, again, we must remember John 3:3: "Except a man be born from above, he cannot see the kingdom of God." Surely seeing the kingdom of God is the act of faith and, if so, such faith is impossible without regeneration. Hence regeneration must be prior to faith. We can affirm then on these grounds that the order is regeneration, faith, justification.

This does not settle the question as to the order in connection with calling and regeneration. Is regeneration prior to effectual calling or is the reverse the case? There are arguments which could be pleaded in favor of the priority of regeneration. No great issue would be at stake in adopting that order, that is to say, the order, regeneration, calling, faith, justification, glorification. There is, however, one weighty consideration (a consideration that will be developed later on), namely, that in the teaching of Scripture it is calling that is given distinct emphasis and prominence as that act of God whereby sinners are translated from darkness to light and ushered into the fellowship of Christ. This feature of New Testament teaching creates the distinct impression that salvation in actual possession takes its start from an efficacious summons on the part of God and that this summons, since it is God's summons, carries in its bosom all of the operative efficacy by which it is made effective. It is calling and not regeneration that possesses that character. Hence there is more to be said for the priority of calling.

If then we have the following elements and in the following order: calling, regeneration, faith, justification, and glorification, we have really settled all that is of basic importance to the question. The other steps can be readily filled in and put in their proper place. Repentance is the twin sister of faith — we cannot think of the one without the other, and so repentance would be conjoined with faith. Conversion is simply another name for repentance and faith conjoined and would therefore be inclosed in repentance and faith. Adoption would obviously come after justification — we could not think of one being adopted into the family of God without first of all being accepted by God and made an heir of eternal life. Sanctification is a process that begins, we might say, in regeneration, finds its basis in justification, and derives its energizing grace from the union with Christ which is effected in effectual calling. Being a continuous process rather than a momentary act like calling, regeneration, justification and adoption, it is proper that it should be placed after adoption in the order of application. Perseverance is the concomitant and complement of the sanctifying process and might conveniently be placed either before or after sanctification.

With all these considerations in view, the order in the application of redemption is found to be, calling, regeneration, faith and repentance, justification, adoption, sanctification, perseverance, glorification. When this order is carefully weighed we find that there is a logic which evinces and brings into clear focus the governing principle of salvation in all of its aspects, the grace of God in its sovereignty and efficacy. Salvation is of the Lord in its application as well as in its conception and accomplishment.

CHAPTER II

Effectual Calling

In the preceding chapter it was stated that there are good reasons for believing that the application of redemption begins with God's effectual call to sinners who are dead in trespasses and sins. It was admitted that considerations in favor of placing regeneration first could be pleaded and that no great issue would be at stake if that were done. The reasons for placing God's call first will become more apparent after we have set forth the Biblical teaching on the subject of the effectual call.

We may properly speak of a call which is not in itself effectual. That is often spoken of as the universal call of the gospel. The overtures of grace in the gospel addressed to all men without distinction are very real and we must maintain that doctrine with all its implications for God's grace, on the one hand, and for man's responsibility and privilege, on the other. It is not improper to refer to that universal overture as a universal call. It is highly probable that it is this call that is referred to in Matthew 22:14: "Many are called, but few are chosen." And there are several texts in the Old Testament which could be appealed to in support of this conclusion.

But it is very striking that in the New Testament the terms for calling, when used specifically with reference to salvation, are almost uniformly applied, not to the universal call of the gospel, but to the call that ushers men into a state of salvation and is therefore effectual. There is scarcely an instance where the terms are used to designate the indiscriminate overture of grace in the gospel of Christ. Hence the all but uniform meaning is that which is fixed by such well-known passages as Romans 8:30: "Whom he did predestinate, them he also called," 1 Corinthians 1:9: "God is faithful, by whom ye were called into the fellowship of his Son," 2 Peter 1:10: "Wherefore the rather, brethren, give diligence to make your calling and election sure" (cf. Rom. 1:6-7; 1 Cor. 1:26). This is the reason why we generally speak of this calling as effectual. With scarcely an exception the New Testament means by the words "call," "called," "calling" nothing less than the call which is efficacious unto salvation.

The Author. In connection with the subject of this caption there are particularly two things to be noted.

1. God is the author. "God is faithful, by whom ye were called into the fellowship of his Son Jesus Christ our Lord" (1 Cor. 1:9). "Be thou partaker of the afflictions of the gospel according to the power of God, who saved us and called us with a holy calling" (2 Tim. 1:8-9). In this respect calling is an act of God's grace and power just as regeneration, justification, and adoption are. We do not call ourselves, we do not set ourselves apart by sovereign volition any more than we regenerate, justify, or adopt ourselves. Calling is an act of God and of God alone. This fact should make us keenly aware how dependent we are upon the sovereign grace of God in the application of redemption. If calling is the initial step in our becoming actual partakers of salvation, the fact that God is its author forcefully reminds us that the pure sovereignty of God's work of salvation is not suspended at the point of application any more than at the point of design and objective accomplishment. We may not like this doctrine. But, if so, it is because we are averse to the grace of God and wish to ar-

rogate to ourselves the prerogative that belongs to God. And we know where that disposition had its origin.

2. It is God the Father who is the specific agent in the effectual call. This aspect of Biblical teaching we are too liable to overlook. We think of the Father as the person of the trinity who planned salvation and as the specific agent in election. And we think properly when we do so. But we fail to discern other emphases of Scripture and we do dishonor to the Father when we think of him simply as planning salvation and redemption. The Father is not far removed from the effectuation of that which he designed in his eternal counsel and accomplished in the death of his Son; he comes into the most intimate relation to his people in the application of redemption by being the specific and particular actor in the inception of such application.

The evidence to support this is copious and conclusive. When Paul says, "Moreover whom he did predestinate, them he also called" (Rom. 8:30), it is obvious that the author of predestination is the author of the call. And in the preceding verse the author of predestination is distinguished from the person who is called "his Son" — "whom he did foreknow, he also did predestinate to be conformed to the image of his Son." Only of the Father can it be said that he predestinated to be conformed to the image of his Son for the simple reason that only in respect of the Father is the Son the Son. Likewise in I Corinthians 1:9, when Paul says, "God is faithful, by whom ye were called into the fellowship of his Son," the same inference holds because the person who calls is distinguished from the person into whose fellowship the called are ushered, and the person thus distinguished is the person who stands to the Son in the relation of Father. This can be none other than the first person of the Godhead, here designated, as frequently in the New Testament, by the personal name "God." Other passages are equally clear to this effect (see Gal. 1:15; Eph. 1:17-18; 2 Tim. 1:9). It may also be proper in this connection to be reminded of 1 John 3:1: "Behold what manner of love the Father hath bestowed upon us that we should be called sons of God." It is very likely that the word "called" means more than merely "named" and refers to the effectual action of God the Father whereby we are "called" to be sons of God.

It is God the Father specifically and by way of eminence who calls effectually by his grace.

The Nature. We often fail to grasp the rich meaning of biblical terms because in common usage the same words have suffered a great deal of attrition. This is true in respect of the word "call." If we are to understand the strength of this word, as used in this connection, we must use the word "summons." The action by which God makes his people the partakers of redemption is that of summons. And since it is God's summons it is efficacious summons.

We do not ordinarily associate with the word "summons" the efficacy that is requisite for compliance with that summons. A summons issued by a court does not of itself empower us to appear in court. It gives us warrant to appear and it requires us to appear but it does not actually bring us into court. That depends on our strength and will. Or, perchance, it depends on the force applied by the executive officers if we are apprehended and compelled to appear. It is wholly otherwise with God's summons. The summons is invested with the efficacy by which we are delivered to the destination intended — we are effectively ushered into the fellowship of Christ. There is something determinate about God's call; by his sovereign power and grace it cannot fail of accomplishment. God calls the things that be not as though they were (*cf.* Rom. 4:17).

Co-ordinate with this fact of efficacy is the truth of its immutability. "The gifts and the calling of God are without repentance" (Rom. 11:29). Nothing clinches the argument for this feature of the call more clearly than the teaching of Romans 8:28-30 where the call is stated to be according to God's purpose and finds its place in the center of that unbreakable chain of events which has its beginning in the divine foreknowledge and its consummation in glorification. This is just saying that the effectual call insures perseverance because it is grounded in the security of God's purpose and grace.

The call is also a high, holy, and heavenly calling (Phil. 3:14; 2 Tim. 1:9; Heb. 3:1). It is high, holy, and heavenly in its origin and in its destiny. But it is probably the character of the calling that is particularly stressed. The life into which the people of God are ushered is one that separates them from the fellowship of this present evil world and imparts to them a character consonant with that consecration. If we find ourselves at home in the ungodliness, lust, and filth of this present world, it is because we have not been called effectually by God's grace. The called are "the called of Jesus Christ" (Rom. 1:6), called to be his property and peculiar possession, and therefore they are "called to be saints" (Rom. 1:7). The called must exemplify in their conduct the calling by which they have been called and have no fellowship with the unfruitful works of darkness. Here we have a series of considerations which presses home the obligations which are intrinsic to God's call. The sovereignty and efficacy of the call do not relax human responsibility but rather ground and confirm that responsibility. The magnitude of the grace enhances the obligation. This is the effect of Paul's exhortation, "I, the prisoner in the Lord, beseech you therefore to walk worthily of the calling wherewith you have been called" (Eph. 4:1).

The Pattern. When we do something with intelligence and wisdom we do it with design and according to plan. We build a house according to the architectural blueprint. We make a suit according to pattern. How preeminently true this is of

God himself. Execution with God is the perfect fulfillment of the designed plan. And that plan is his own purpose and grace given in Christ Jesus before times eternal (2 Tim. 1:9; cf. Rom. 8:28). The following features of this pattern need to be noted.

1. It is the pattern of determinate purpose. When God calls men and women it is not on the moment of haphazard, arbitrary, sudden decision. God's thought has been occupied with this event from times eternal. Hence the moment and all the circumstances are fixed by his own counsel and will.

2. It is eternal. Have we sufficiently entertained the marvel that God's thought and interest and purpose have been occupied from eternity with the grace which is actually bestowed in time? We cannot think in terms of eternity; we have no eternal thought. Only God's thought possesses that attribute because he alone is eternal. When we try to think of eternity we realize the limits of our understanding and we are reminded that eternity is incomprehensible to us. But we must think of eternity and think of it in such a way that the more we are aware of the limits of our understanding the more enhanced becomes our appreciation of the marvel of God's eternal purpose and grace.

3. It is in Christ the pattern is devised — "according to his own purpose and grace which was given to us in Christ Jesus" (2 Tim. 1:9). Under an earlier caption emphasis was placed upon the truth that God the Father by way of eminence is the agent in the effectual call. We must not think of the Father as removed from the people of God in the application of redemption — he is the specific agent in its inception. But we must also remember that the call is never apart from Christ. Nothing advertises this more clearly than the fact that the counsel of the Father in the eternal ages with respect to the call, the conceiving and proposing of it, was not apart from Christ. The people of God are not contemplated even in the purpose of grace apart from Christ (cf. Rom. 8:29; Eph. 1:4).

We have here an index to the perfect harmony and conjunction of the persons of the Godhead in those operations which are embraced in the economy of salvation. It is co-ordination that goes back to the fountainhead of salvation.

The Priority. As was stated already no great issue of theological or exegetical consequence would be at stake if regeneration were regarded as logically prior to calling. But there are reasons for thinking that calling is the first step in the application of redemption.

1. It is calling that is represented in Scripture as that act of God by which we are *actually* united to Christ (cf. 1 Cor. 1:9). And surely union with Christ is that which unites us to the inwardly operative grace of God. Regeneration is the beginning of inwardly operative saving grace.

2. Calling is a sovereign act of God alone and we must not define it in terms of the response which is elicited in the heart and mind and will of the person called. When this is taken into account, it is more reasonable to construe regeneration as that which is wrought inwardly by God's grace in order that we may yield to God's call the appropriate and necessary response. In that case the new birth would come after the call and prior to the response on our part. It provides the link between the call and the response on the part of the person called.

3. It is not by any means likely that Paul in Romans 8:28-30, in setting forth the outlines of the order followed in the application of redemption, would begin that enumeration with an act of God which is other than the first in order. In other words, it is altogether likely that he would begin with the first, just as he ends with the last. This argument is strengthened by the consideration that he traces salvation to its ultimate source in the election of God. Surely he traces the application of redemption to its beginning when he says, "whom he did predestinate them he also called." And so calling would be the initial act of application.

4. All the aspects of the application of redemption find their explanation in God's eternal purpose of grace — they are all in accordance with God's eternal purpose. But in the New Testament particular emphasis is placed upon the fact that calling is in accordance with this eternal purpose (cf. Rom. 8:28-30; 2 Tim. 1:9). It is proper to infer that this emphasis appears for the very reason that the dependence of the whole process of application upon the eternal purpose could not be more clearly exhibited than by showing that the initial act of application proceeds from the eternal purpose of grace.

For such reasons as these there is good warrant for the conclusion that the application of redemption begins with the sovereign and efficacious summons by which the people of God are ushered into the fellowship of Christ and union with him to the end that they may become partakers of all the grace and virtue which reside in him as Redeemer, Savior, and Lord.

CHAPTER III

Regeneration

We have found that the application of redemption begins with an effectual call by which God the Father ushers men into the fellowship of his Son. An *effectual* call, however, must carry along with it the appropriate response on the part of the person called. It is God who calls but it is not God who answers the call; it is the person to whom the call is addressed. And this response must enlist the exercise of the heart and mind and will of the person concerned. It is at this point that we are compelled to ask the question: how can a person who is dead in trespasses and sins, whose mind is enmity against God, and who cannot do that which is well-pleasing to God answer a call to the fellowship of Christ? Fellowship is never one-sided; it is always mutual. Hence the fellowship of Christ must involve the embrace of Christ in faith and love. And how can a person whose heart is depraved and whose mind is enmity against God embrace him who is the supreme manifestation of the glory of God? The answer to this question is that the believing and loving response which the calling requires is a moral and spiritual impossibility on the part of one who is dead in trespasses and sins. "They that are in the flesh cannot please God" (Rom. 8:8). And our Savior himself gives unequivocal expression to this impossibility when he says: "No one can come unto me except the Father who hath sent me draw him"; "No one can come unto me except it were given to him of the Father" (John 6:44, 65). The fact is that there is a complete incongruity between the glory and virtue to which sinners are called, on the one hand, and the moral and spiritual condition of the called, on the other. How is this incongruity to be resolved and the impossibility overcome?

It is the glory of the gospel of God's grace that it provides for this incongruity. God's call, since it is effectual, carries with it the operative grace whereby the person called is enabled to answer the call and to embrace Jesus Christ as he is freely offered in the gospel. God's grace reaches down to the lowest depths of our need and meets all the exigencies of the moral and spiritual impossiblity which inheres in our depravity and inability. And that grace is the grace of regeneration. It is when we take into account God's recreative power and grace that the contradiction between the call of God and the sinful condition of the called is resolved. "A new heart also will I give you, and a new spirit will I put within you" (Ezek. 36:26). God effects a change which is radical and all-pervasive, a change which cannot be explained in terms of any combination, permutation, or accumulation of human resources, a change which is nothing less than a new creation by him who calls the things that be not as though they were, who spake and it was done, who commanded and it stood fast. This, in a word, is regeneration.

There is no passage of Scripture more relevant than the words of our Lord himself to Nicodemus. They are familiar words, but how frequently their most obvious meaning is ignored or distorted. The mode of regeneration is truly mysterious and to this Jesus points in this passage when he says, "The wind bloweth where it listeth, and thou hearest the sound thereof, but canst not tell whence it cometh, and whither it goeth: so is every one that is born of the Spirit"

(John 3:8). But there are plain lessons respecting the necessity and the character of the new birth which lie on the face of Jesus' teaching here.

When our Lord says that the supernatural birth spoken of is indispensable to seeing and entering into the kingdom of God he surely means by "seeing" the spiritual discernment of which Paul speaks in 1 Corinthians 2:14 and by "entering into" he refers to that by which we become actual members of the kingdom of God and therefore partakers of the blessing which membership entails. We may focus attention upon verse 5: "Except one be born of water and of the Spirit, he cannot enter into the kingdom of God."

A good deal of difference of judgment has turned on the question: what did Jesus mean by "water" in this text? Some think Jesus referred to Christian baptism as the laver of regeneration, and those who believe in baptismal regeneration like to appeal to this text in support of that doctrine.

At the outset it should be noted that Jesus does not say baptism; he says water. We must not take it for granted that he means baptism unless there is some compelling reason for thinking that in using the word "water" he must have been referring to the water of baptism. But there is no need to regard the word "water" in this text as referring to the rite of baptism and there are good reasons for thinking that it has another import and reference. We should keep in view the situation in which Jesus spoke these words. He was engaged in a dialogue with Nicodemus on an intensely religious question. In terms of this conversation nothing is more reasonable and natural than to suppose that Jesus wanted to convey to Nicodemus an idea of religious import which would be directly relevant to the subject of interest. Now what religious idea would we expect to be conveyed to the mind of Nicodemus by the use of the word "water"? Of course, the idea associated with the *religious* use of water in that religious tradition and practice which provided the very context of Nicodemus' life and profession. And that is just saying the religious import of water in the Old Testament, in the rites of Judaism, and in contemporary practice. When we say this there is one answer. The religious use of water, that is to say, the religiously symbolic meaning of water, pointed in one direction, and that direction is purification. All the relevant considerations would conspire to convey to Nicodemus that message. And that message would be focused in his mind in one central thought, the indispensable necessity of purification for entrance into the kingdom of God.

It was characteristic of Jesus' teaching to lay his finger directly upon the characteristic sin and need of those with whom he was dealing. The characteristic sin of the pharisees was self-complacency and self-righteousness. What they needed was to be convinced of their own pollution and the need of radical purification. It is this lesson that the expression "born of water" would have conveyed most effectively. Entrance into the kingdom of God could only be secured by purification from the defilement of sin. The water of purification is as it were the womb out of which must emerge that new life which gives entrance into and fits for membership in the kingdom of God. This is the purificatory aspect of regeneration. Regeneration must negate the past as well as reconstitute for the future. It must cleanse from sin as well as recreate in righteousness.

There can be no question but "born of the Spirit" refers to birth of the Holy Spirit (cf. verse 8 and John 1:13; 1 John 2:29; 3:9; 4:7; 5:1, 4, 18). It is birth therefore of divine and supernatural character. And it is such because the Holy Spirit is the source and agent of it.

It needs to be particularly noted what is implied in this familiar expression "born of the Spirit." It is not quite certain whether the exact meaning of the word rendered "born" is that of begetting or bearing. According to the usage of the New Testament it could be either. If it is the former, then the thought is patterned after the action of the father in human procreation — the man begets. If it is the latter, then the thought is patterned after the action of the mother — the woman bears, the child is born of the mother. We cannot be certain which of these more precise meanings is in view here. But it makes no essential difference to the truth expressed. Whether we think of being begotten of the Spirit or of being born of the Spirit one thing is certain — we are instructed by our Lord that for entrance into the kingdom of God we are wholly dependent upon the action of the Holy Spirit, an action of the Holy Spirit which is compared to that on the part of our parents by which we were born into the world. We are as dependent upon the Holy Spirit as we are upon the action of our parents in connection with our natural birth. We were not begotten by our father because we decided to be. And we were not born of our mother because we decided to be. We were simply begotten and we were born. We did not decide to be born. This is the simple but too frequently overlooked truth which our Lord here teaches us. We do not have spiritual perception of the kingdom of God nor do we enter into it because we willed to or decided to. If this privilege is ours it is because the Holy Spirit willed it and here all rests upon the Holy Spirit's decision and action. He begets or bears when and where he pleases. Is this not the burden of verse 8? Jesus there compares the action of the Spirit to the action of the wind. The wind blows — this serves to illustrate the factuality, the certainty, the efficacy of the Spirit's action. The wind blows where it wills — this enforces the sovereignty of the Spirit's action. The wind is not at our beck and call; neither is the regenerative operation of the Spirit. "Thou canst not tell whence it cometh, and whither it goeth" — the Spirit's work is mysterious. All points up the sovereignty, efficacy, and inscrutability of the Holy Spirit's work in regeneration.

It is the Holy Spirit who effects this change. He effects it because he is the source of it. He effects it by the mode of generation. And since he effects it by this mode he is the sole author and active agent.

It has often been said that we are passive in regeneration. This is a true and proper statement. For it is simply the precipitate of what our Lord has taught us here. We may not like it. We may recoil against it. It may not fit into our way of thinking and it may not accord with the time-worn expressions which are the coin of our evangelism. But if we recoil against it, we do well to remember that this recoil is recoil against Christ. And what shall we answer when we appear before him whose truth we rejected and with whose gospel we tampered? But blessed be God that the gospel of Christ is one of sovereign, efficacious, irresistible regeneration. If it were not the case that in regeneration we are passive, the subjects of an action of which God alone is the agent, there would be no gospel at all. For unless God by sovereign, operative grace had turned our enmity to love and our disbelief to faith we would never yield the response of faith and love.

John 3:5 sets forth the two aspects from which the new birth must be viewed — it purges away the defilement of our hearts and it recreates in newness of life. The two elements of this text — "born of water" and "born of the Spirit" — correspond to the two elements of the Old Testament counterpart: "Then will I sprinkle clean water upon you, and ye shall be clean: from all your filthiness, and from all your idols, will I cleanse you. A new heart also will I give you, and a new spirit will I put within you: and I will take away the stony heart out of your flesh, and I will give you an heart of flesh" (Ezek. 36:25-26). This passage we may properly regard as the Old Testament parallel of John 3:5 and there is neither reason nor warrant for placing any other interpretation upon "born of water" than that of Ezekiel 36:25: "Then will I sprinkle clean water upon you, and ye shall be clean." These elements, the purificatory and the renovatory, must not be regarded as separable events. They are simply the aspects which are constitutive of this total change by which the called of God are translated from death to life and from the kingdom of Satan into God's kingdom, a change which provides for all the exigencies of our past condition and the demands of the new life in Christ, a change which removes the contradiction of sin and fits for the fellowship of God's Son.

It was the apostle John who recorded for us our Lord's discourse to Nicodemus. John had learned its lesson well and particularly the lesson that regeneration is the act of God and of God alone, that men are born again "not of blood, nor of the will of the flesh, nor of the will of man, but of God" (John 1:13). He has inscribed this teaching indelibly upon his first epistle, also. Explicit reference to regeneration appears in that epistle on several occasions (1 John 2:29; 3:9; 4:7; 5:1, 4, 18). The leading emphasis in these passages is upon the fact that there is an invariable concomitance or co-ordination of regeneration and other fruits of grace. In 2:29 it is the concomitance (togetherness) of the divine begetting and doing righteousness; in 3:9 of the divine begetting, on the one hand, and not doing sin and incapacity to sin, on the other; in 4:7 of the divine begetting and love; in 5:1 of the divine begetting and believing that Jesus is the Christ; in 5:4 of the divine begetting and overcoming the world; in 5:18 of divine begetting and not sinning and immunity to the touch of the evil one. As we shall see later, this is a very significant emphasis and warns us against any view of regeneration which abstracts it from the other elements of the application of redemption.

In most of these passages all that is expressly stated is this truth of the invariable concomitance of regeneration and these other blessings of grace. But in 3:9 we are expressly informed of something else, namely, the relation which regeneration sustains to the other particular graces mentioned in that text. "Everyone who is begotten of God does not do sin; because his seed abides in him; and he cannot sin, because he is begotten of God." Not only is it stated that the person who is born again does not do sin, but we are also informed of the reason why he does not sin. He does not sin because God's seed abides in him. Now this abiding seed alludes clearly to the divine impartation which took place in the divine begetting. It is this divine begetting with its abiding consequence that is the *cause* of not doing sin. Hence regeneration is logically and causally prior to the not doing sin. And, again, John tells us that "he cannot sin because he is begotten of God," an express statement to the effect that regeneration is the *cause* why this person cannot sin. So the reason why a person cannot sin is that that person is regenerated — the order cannot be reversed. In this verse, therefore, we are informed that regeneration is the source and explantion of the breach with sin which is characteristic of every regenerate person.

We have found thus in 1 John 3:9 a principle which must apply to the other texts cited in this epistle, even though the principle is not expressly mentioned in these other texts. The inference is confirmed when we compare 3:9 with 5:18. The latter reads: "We know that everyone who is begotten of God does not sin, but he who has been begotten of God keeps himself, and the evil one does not touch him." The thought here is very closely similar to that in 3:9. In fact it is in part identical, with a slight variation of terms. If what we have found to be true in 3:9 applies to what is taught in 3:9, it must also apply to what is taught in 5:18. And that means that the reason why a person does not sin is that he is begotten of God and the reason why the evil one does not touch a person is that he is begotten of God. Regeneration is the logical and causal explanation of abstinence from sin and freedom from the touch of the evil one.

Of course it is not our purpose now to determine what this freedom from sin, this incapacity to sin, and this immunity to the invasion of the evil one precisely mean. All we are interested in at present is simply to establish the relation which regeneration sustains to these characteristics of the regenerate person.

We are forced to the conclusion, therefore, on the basis of 3:9 and 5:18, that the relation established in these two texts applies to all the others also. In 2:29, we must infer, that the reason why the person in view does righteousness is that he is begotten of God. And likewise in the others. In 4:7 regeneration must be regarded as the cause of love, in 5:1 the cause of belief that Jesus is the Christ, in 5:4 the cause of overcoming the world. We have therefore a whole catalogue of virtues — belief that Jesus is the Christ, overcoming the world, abstinence from sin, self-control, incapacity to sin, freedom from the touch of the evil one, doing righteousness, love to God and one's neighbor. And they are all the fruit of regeneration. It should be noted how comprehensive and representative this catalogue is. It covers the wide range of the virtue demanded by the high calling of God in Christ Jesus. In the order in which they have been stated above, as Bengel expressed it in another connection, faith leads the band and love brings up the rear.

It should be specially noted that even faith that Jesus is the Christ is the effect of regeneration. This is, of course, a clear implication of John 3:3-8. But John the apostle here takes pains to make that plain. Regeneration is the beginning of all saving grace *in us*, and all saving grace in exercise on our part proceeds from the fountain of regeneration. We are not born again by faith or repentance or conversion; we repent and believe because we have been regenerated. No one can say in truth that Jesus is the Christ except by regeneration of the Spirit and that is one of the ways by which the Holy Spirit glorifies Christ. The embrace of Christ in faith is the first evidence of regeneration and only thus may we know that we have been regenerated.

The priority of regeneration might create the impression that a person could be regenerated and yet not converted. These passages in 1 John should correct any such misapprehension. We need to remember again that the leading emphasis in these passages is the invariable concomitance of regeneration and the other graces mentioned. "Everyone who is begotten of God does not do sin, for his seed remains in him; and he cannot sin, because he is begotten of God" (3:9). "Everyone who is begotten of God overcomes the world; and this is the victory which has overcome the world, even our faith" (5:4). "Everyone who is begotten of God does not sin, but he who has been begotten of God keep himself, and the wicked one does not touch him" (5:18). When we put these texts together they expressly state that every regenerate person has been delivered from the power of sin, overcomes the world by the faith of Christ, and exercises that self-control by which he is no longer the slave of sin and of the evil one. That means, when reduced to its simplest terms, that the regenerate person is converted and exercises faith and repentance. We must not think of regeneration as something which can be abstracted from the saving exercises which are its effects. Hence we shall have to conclude that in the other passages (2:29; 4:7; 5:1) the fruits mentioned — doing righteousness, the love and knowledge of God, believing that Jesus is the Christ — are just as necessarily the accompaniments of regeneration as are the fruits mentioned in 3:9; 5:4, 18. This simply means that all of the graces mentioned in these passages are the consequences of regeneration and not only consequences which sooner or later follow upon regeneration, but fruits which are inseparable from regeneration. We are warned and advised, therefore, that while regeneration is the action of God and of God alone we must never conceive of this action as separable from the activities of saving grace on our part which are the necessary and appropriate effects of God's grace in us. The apostle John had learned of his Lord and what he teaches in his epistle is, in other terms, exactly what Jesus taught in his discourse to Nicodemus. If it is true that no one enters the kingdom of God except by regeneration (John 3:3, 5), it is also just as true that everyone who is born again has entered into the kingdom of God. If regeneration is the way of entrance, then those regenerated have entered and, having entered, they see the kingdom of God and are members of it. This is again the pointed lesson of Jesus in John 3:6: "that which is born of the Spirit is spirit," that is to say, the person born of the Holy Spirit is indwelt and directed by the Holy Spirit. The regenerate person cannot live in sin and be unconverted. And neither can he live any longer in neutral abstraction. He is immediately a member of the kingdom of God, he is spirit, and his action and behavior must be consonant with that new citizenship. In the language of the apostle Paul, "if any man be in Christ, he is a new creature; the old things have passed away, behold they have become new" (2 Cor. 5:17). There are numerous other considerations derived from the Scripture which confirm this great truth that regeneration is such a radical, pervasive, and efficacious transformation that it immediately registers itself in the conscious activity of the person concerned in the exercises of faith and repentance and new obedience. Far too frequently the conception entertained of conversion is so superficial and beggarly that it completely fails to take account of the momentous change of which conversion is the fruit. And the whole notion of what is involved in the application of redemption becomes so attenuated that it has little or no resemblance to that which the gospel teaches. Regeneration is at the basis of all change in heart and life. It is a stupendous change because it is God's recreative act. A cheap and tawdry evangelism has tended to rob the gospel which it proclaims of that invincible power which is the glory of the gospel of sovereign grace. May the church come to think and live again in terms of the gospel which is *the power of God* unto salvation.

CHAPTER IV

Faith and Repentance

Regeneration is inseparable from its effects and one of the effects is faith. Without regeneration it is morally and spiritually impossible for a person to believe in Christ, but when a person is regenerated it is morally and spiritually impossible for that person not to believe. Jesus said, "All that the Father giveth me shall come to me" (John 6:37), and he was referring in this case surely to the giving of the Father in the efficacious drawing of the Father mentioned in the same context (John 6:44, 65). Regeneration is the renewing of the heart and mind, and the renewed heart and mind must act according to their nature.

Faith

Regeneration is the act of God and of God alone. But faith is not the act of God; it is not God who believes in Christ for salvation, it is the sinner. It is by God's grace that a person is able to believe but faith is an activity on the part of the person and of him alone. In faith we receive and rest upon Christ alone for salvation.

It might be said: this is a strange mixture. God alone regenerates. We alone believe. And we believe in Christ alone for salvation. But this is precisely the way it is. It is well for us to appreciate all that is implied in the combination, for it is God's way of salvation and it expresses his supreme wisdom and grace. In salvation God does not deal with us as machines; he deals with us as persons and therefore salvation brings the whole range of our activity within its scope. By grace we are saved through faith (cf. Eph. 2:8).

If we are to have a better understanding of what faith is we must examine it as to its *warrant* and as to its *nature*.

The Warrant. Faith, as we shall see later, is a whole-souled movement of self-commitment to Christ for salvation from sin and its consequences. It is not unnecessary to ask the question: what warrant does a lost sinner have to commit himself to Christ? How may he know that he will be accepted? How does he know that Christ is able to save? How does he know that this confidence is not misplaced? How does he know that Christ is willing to save *him*? These are urgent questions, perhaps not urgent for the person who has no true conception of the issues at stake or of the gravity of his lost condition, but exceedingly urgent and pertinent for the person convicted of sin and in whose heart burns the reality and realization of the wrath of God against sin. There are the following facts which constitute the warrant of faith.

1. *The Universal Offer of the Gospel.* This offer may be regarded from several viewpoints. It may be regarded as invitation, as demand, as promise, and as overture. But from whatever angle we may view it, it is full, free, and unrestricted. The appeals of the gospel cover the whole range of divine prerogative and of human interest. God entreats, he invites, he commands, he calls, he presents the overture of mercy and grace, and he does this to all without distinction or discrimination.

It may surprise us that this universal offer should receive such prominence in the Old Testament. Under the Old Testament the revelation of God's saving grace was given to a chosen people and to them were committed the oracles of God. The psalmist could sing, "In Judah is God known: his name is great in Israel. In Salem also is his tabernacle, and his dwelling place in Zion" (Ps. 76:1-2). And Jesus could say of this Old Testament period, "Salvation is of the Jews" (John 4:22). There was a middle wall of partition between Jew and Gentile. But it is in the Old Testament we find such an appeal as this: "There is no God else beside me; a just God and a Saviour; there is none beside me. Look unto me, and be ye saved, all the ends of the earth: for I am God and there is none else" (Isa. 45:21-22). Again we read: "As I live saith the Lord God, I have no pleasure in the death of the wicked; but that the wicked turn from his way and live: turn ye, turn ye from your evil ways; for why will ye die, O house of Israel?" (Ezek. 33:11; cf. 18:23, 32). Here is the most emphatic negation — "I have no pleasure in the death of the wicked," affirmation "but that the wicked turn from his way and live," asseveration — "as I live saith the Lord God," exhortation — "turn ye, turn ye from your evil ways," protestation — "why will ye die?"

If there is universality of exhortation and appeal when God's covenant grace was concentrated in Israel, how much more apparent must this be when there is now no longer Jew nor Gentile and the middle wall of partition is broken down, when the gospel is proclaimed in terms of Jesus' commission, "Go ye therefore and disciple all the nations" (Matt. 28:19). The words of Jesus are redolent of this indiscriminate invitation, "Come unto me, all ye that labour and are heavy laden, and I will give you rest" (Matt. 11:28); "him that cometh unto me I will in no wise cast out" (John 6:37). And the words of the apostle are unmistakably clear: "And the times of this ignorance God winked at, but now he commandeth men that they should all everywhere repent, inasmuch as he hath appointed a day in which he will judge the world in righteousness, by the man whom he hath ordained, having given assurance unto all men in that he hath raised him from the dead" (Acts 17:30-31). It is not simply that God entreats men everywhere that they should turn and repent; he commands them to do so. It is a charge invested with the authority and majesty of his sovereignty as Lord of all. The sovereign imperative of God is brought to bear upon the overture of grace. And that is the end of all contention. From his command to all no one is excluded.

2. *The All-Sufficiency and Suitability of the Savior Presented.* Christ presented himself in the glory of his person and in the sufficiency of his saviorhood when he said, "Come unto me, all ye that labour and are heavy laden, and I will give you rest" (Matt. 11:28), and again, "Him that cometh unto me I will in no wise cast out" (John 6:37). It is this truth that is enunciated when it is written, "Wherefore he is able to save them to the uttermost that come unto God by him, seeing he ever liveth to make intercession for them" (Heb.7:25). The sufficiency of his saviorhood rests upon the work he accomplished once for all when he died upon the cross and rose again in triumphant power. But it resides in the efficacy and perfection of his continued activity at the right hand of God. It is because he continues ever and has an unchangeable priesthood that he is able to save them that come unto him and to give them eternal life. When Christ is presented to lost men in the proclamation of the gospel, it is as Savior he is presented, as one who ever continues to be the embodiment of the salvation he has once for all accomplished. It is not the possibility of salvation that is offered to lost men but the Savior himself and therefore salvation full and perfect. There is no imperfection in the salvation offered and there is no restriction to its overture — it is full, free, and unrestricted. And this is the warrant of faith.

The faith of which we are now speaking is not the belief that we have been saved but trust in Christ in order that we may be saved. And it is of paramount concern to know that Christ is presented to all without distinction to the end that they may entrust themselves to him for salvation. The gospel offer is not restricted to the elect or even to those for whom Christ died. And the warrant of faith is not the conviction that we are elect or that we are among those for whom, strictly speaking, Christ died but the fact that Christ, in the glory of his person, in the perfection of his finished work, and in the efficacy of his exalted activity as King and Savior, is presented to us in the full, free, and unrestricted overture of the gospel. It is not as persons convinced of our election nor as persons convinced that we are the special objects of God's love that we commit ourselves to him but as lost sinners. We entrust ourselves to him not because we believe we have been saved but as lost sinners in order that we may be saved. It is to us in our lost condition that the warrant of faith is given and the warrant is not restricted or circumscribed in any way. In the warrant of faith the rich mercy of God is proffered to the lost and the promise of grace is certified by the veracity and faithfulness of God. This is the ground upon which a lost sinner may commit himself to Christ in full confidence that he will be saved. And no sinner to whom the gospel comes is excluded from the divine warrant for such confidence.

The Nature. There are three things that need to be said about the nature of faith. Faith is *knowledge, conviction,* and *trust.*

1. *Knowledge.* It might seem very confusing to say that faith is knowledge. For is is not one thing to know, another thing to believe? This is partly true. Sometimes we must distinguish between faith and knowledge and place them in contrast to each other. But there is a knowledge that is indispensable to faith. In our ordinary human relations do we trust a person of whom we know nothing, Especially when that for which we trust him is of grave importance for us we must know a good deal regarding his identity and his character. How much

more must this be the case with that faith which is directed to Christ; for it is faith against all the issues of life and death, of time and eternity. We must know who Christ is, what he has done, and what he is able to do. Otherwise faith would be blind conjecture at the best and foolish mockery at the worst. There must be apprehension of the truth respecting Christ.

Sometimes, indeed, the measure of truth apprehended by the believing person is very small, and we have to appreciate the fact that the faith of some in its initial stages is very elementary. But faith cannot begin in a vacuum of knowledge. Paul reminds us of this very simply when he says, "Faith is of hearing, and hearing of the word of Christ" (Rom. 10:17).

2. *Conviction.* Faith is assent. We must not only know the truth respecting Christ but we must also believe it to be true. It is possible, of course, for us to understand the import of certain propositions of truth and yet not believe these propositions. All disbelief is of this character, and the more intelligently the import of the truths concerned is understood the more violent may be the disbelief. A person who rejects the virgin birth may understand well what the doctrine of the virgin birth is and for that very reason reject it. But we are now dealing not with disbelief or unbelief but with faith and this obviously implies that the truths known are also accepted as true.

The conviction which enters into faith is not only an assent to the truth respecting Christ but also a recognition of the exact correspondence that there is between the truth of Christ and our deeds as lost sinners. What Christ is as Savior perfectly dovetails our deepest and most ultimate need. This is just saying that Christ's sufficiency as Savior meets the desperateness and hopelessness of our sin and misery. It is conviction which engages, therefore, our greatest interest and which registers the verdict: Christ is exactly suited to all that I am in my sin and misery and to all that I should aspire to be by God's grace. Christ fits in perfectly to the totality of our situation in its sin, guilt, misery, and ill-desert.

3. *Trust.* Faith is knowledge passing into conviction, and it is conviction passing into confidence. Faith cannot stop short of self-commitment to Christ, a transference of reliance upon ourselves and all human resources to reliance upon Christ alone for salvation. It is a receiving and resting upon him. It is here that the most characteristic act of faith appears; it is engagement of person to person, the engagement of the sinner as lost to the person of the Savior able and willing to save. Faith, after all, is not belief of propositions of truth respecting the Savior, however essential an ingredient of faith such belief is. Faith is trust in a person, the person of Christ, the Son of God and Savior of the lost. It is entrustment of ourselves to him. It is not simply believing him; it is believing in him and on him.

The Reformers laid special emphasis upon this element of faith. They were opposing the Romish view that faith is assent. It is quite consistent with Romish religion to say that faith is assent. It is the genius of the Romish conception of salvation to intrude mediators between the soul and the Savior — the church, the virgin, the sacraments. On the contrary, it is the glory of the gospel of God's grace that there is one mediator between God and man, the man Christ Jesus. And it was the glory of our Protestant Reformation to discover again the purity of the evangel. The Reformers recognized that the essence of saving faith is to bring the sinner lost and dead in trespasses and sins into direct personal contact with the Savior himself, contact which is nothing less than that of self-commitment to him in all the glory of his person and perfection of his work as he is freely and fully offered in the gospel.

It is to be remembered that the efficacy of faith does not reside in itself. Faith is not something that merits the favor of God. All the efficacy unto salvation resides in the Savior. As one has aptly and truly stated the case, it is not faith that saves but faith in Jesus Christ; strictly speaking, it is not even faith in Christ that saves but Christ that saves through faith. Faith unites us to Christ in the bonds of abiding attachment and entrustment and it is this union which insures that the saving power, grace, and virtue of the Savior become operative in the believer. The specific character of faith is that it looks away from itself and finds its whole interest and object in Christ. He is the absorbing preoccupation of faith.

It is at the point of faith in Christ that our responsibility is engaged to the fullest extent, just as it is in the exercise of faith that our hearts and minds and wills are active to the highest degree. It is not our responsibility to regenerate ourselves. Regeneration is the action of God and of God alone. It is our responsibility to be what regeneration effects. It is our responsibility to be holy. But the act of regeneration does not come within the sphere of our responsible action. Faith does. And we are never relieved of the obligation to believe in Christ to the saving of our souls. The fact that regeneration is the prerequisite of faith in no way relieves us of the responsibility to believe nor does it eliminate the priceless privilege that is ours as Christ and his claims are pressed upon us in full and free overtures of his grace. Our inability is no excuse for our unbelief nor does it provide us with any reason for not believing. As we are presented with Christ in the gospel there is no reason for the rejection of unbelief and all reason demands the entrustment of faith.

Repentance

The question has been discussed: which is prior, faith or repentance? It is an unnecessary question and the insistence that one is prior to the other futile. There is no priority. The faith that is unto salvation is a penitent faith and the repentance that is unto life is a believing repentance. Repentance is admirably defined in the Shorter Catechism. "Repentance unto life is a saving grace, whereby a sinner out of a true sense of his sin, and apprehension of the mercy of God in Christ, doth, with grief and hatred of his sin, turn from it unto God, with full purpose of, and endeavor after new obedience." The interdependence of faith and repentance can be readily seen when we remember that faith is faith in Christ for salvation from sin. But if faith is directed to salvation from sin, there must be hatred of sin and the desire to be saved from it. Such hatred of sin involves repentance which essentially consists in turning from sin unto God. Again, if we remember that repentance is turning from sin unto God, the turning to God implies faith in the mercy of God as revealed in Christ. It is impossible to disentangle faith and repentance. Saving faith is permeated with repentance and repentance is permeated with faith. Regeneration becomes vocal in our minds in the exercises of faith and repentance.

Repentance consists essentially in change of heart and mind and will. The change of heart and mind and will principally respects four things: it is a change of mind respecting God, respecting ourselves, respecting sin, and respecting righteousness. Apart from regeneration our thought of God, of ourselves, of sin, and of righteousness is radically perverted. Regeneration changes our hearts and minds; it radically renews them. Hence there is a radical change in our thinking and feeling. Old things have passed away and all things have become new. It is very important to observe that the faith which is unto salvation is the faith which is accompanied by that change of thought and attitude. Too frequently in evangelical circles and particularly in popular evangelism the momentousness of the change which faith signalizes is not understood or appreciated. There are two fallacies. The one is to put faith out of the context which alone gives it significance, and the other is to think of faith in terms simply of decision and rather cheap decision at that. These fallacies are closely related and condition each other. The emphasis upon repentance and upon the deep-seated change of thought and feeling which it involves is precisely what is necessary to correct this impoverished and soul-destroying conception of faith. The nature of repentance serves to accentuate the urgency of the issues at stake in the demand of the gospel, the cleavage with sin which the acceptance of the gospel entails, and the totally new outlook which the faith of the gospel imparts.

Repentance we must not think of as consisting merely in a change of mind in general; it is very particular and concrete. And since it is a change of mind with reference to sin, it is a change of mind with reference to particular sins, sins in all the particularity and individuality which belong to our sins. It is very easy for us to speak of sin, to be very denunciatory respecting sin, and denunciatory respecting the particular sins of other people and yet not be penitent regarding our own particular sins. The test of repentance is the genuineness and resoluteness of our repentance in respect of our own sins, sins characterized by the aggravations which are peculiar to our own selves. Repentance in the case of the Thessalonians manifested itself in the fact that they turned from idols to serve the living God. It was their idolatry which peculiarly evidenced their alienation from God and it was repentance regarding that that proved the genuineness of their faith and of their hope (I Thess. 1:9, 10).

The gospel is not only that by grace are we saved through faith but it is also the gospel of repentance. When Jesus, after his resurrection, opened the understanding of the disciples that they might understand the Scriptures, he said unto them,

"Thus it is written, and thus it behooved Christ to suffer, and to rise from the dead the third day: and that repentance unto the remission of sins should be preached in his name unto all the nations" (Luke 24:46-47). When Peter had preached to the multitude on the occasion of Pentecost and they were constrained to say, "Men and brethren what shall we do?" Peter replied, "Repent, and be baptized every one of you in the name of Jesus Christ unto the remission of your sins" (Acts 2:37-38). Later on, in like manner, Peter interpreted the exaltation of Christ as exaltation in the capacity of "Prince and Saviour to give repentance to Israel and forgiveness of sins" (Acts 5:31). Could anything certify more clearly that the gospel is the gospel of repentance than the fact that Jesus' heavenly ministry as Savior is one of dispensing repentance unto the forgiveness of sins? Hence Paul, when he gave an account of his own ministry to the elders from Ephesus, said that he testified "both to the Jews and also to the Greeks repentance toward God and faith toward our Lord Jesus" (Acts 20:21). And the writer of the epistle to the Hebrews indicates that "repentance from dead works" is one of the first principles of the doctrine of Christ (Heb. 6:1). It could not be otherwise. The new life in Christ Jesus means that the bands which bind us to the dominion of sin are broken. The believer is dead to sin by the body of Christ, the old man has been crucified that the body of sin might be destroyed, and henceforth he does not serve sin (Rom. 6:2, 6). This breach with the past registers itself in his consciousness in turning from sin unto God "with full purpose of, and endeavor after new obedience."

We see, therefore, that the emphasis which the Scripture places upon faith as the condition of salvation is not to be construed as if faith were the only condition. The various exercises or responses of our spirits have their own peculiar function. Repentance is that which describes the response of turning from sin unto God. This is its specific character just as the specific character of faith is to receive and rest upon Christ alone for salvation. Repentance reminds us that if the faith we profess is a faith that allows us to walk in the ways of this present evil world, in the lust of the flesh, the lust of the eyes, and the pride of life, in the fellowship of the works of darkness, then our faith is but mockery and deception. True faith is suffused with penitence. And just as faith is not only a momentary act but an abiding attitude of trust and confidence directed to the Savior, so repentance results in constant contrition. The broken spirit and the contrite heart are abiding marks of the believing soul. As long as sin remains there must be the consciousness of it and this conviction of our own sinfulness will constrain self-abhorrence, confession, and the plea of forgiveness and cleansing. Christ's blood is the laver of initial cleansing but it is also the fountain to which the believer must continuously repair. It is at the cross of Christ that repentance has its beginning; it is at the cross of Christ that it must continue to pour out its heart in the tears of confession and contrition. The way of sanctification is the way of contrition for the sin of the past and of the present. The Lord forgives our sins, and forgiveness is sealed by the light of his countenance, but we do not forgive ourselves.

CHAPTER V

Justification

The basic religious question is that of our relation to God. How can man be just with God? How can he be right with the Holy One? In our situation, however, the question is much more aggravated. It is not simply, how can man be just with God, but how can sinful man be just with God? In the last analysis sin is always against God, and the essence of sin is to be *against* God. The person who is *against* God cannot be right with God. For if we are against God then God is against us. It could not be otherwise. God cannot be indifferent to or complacent towards that which is the contradiction of himself. His very perfection requires the recoil of righteous indignation. And that is God's wrath. "The wrath of God is revealed from heaven against all ungodliness and unrighteousness of men" (Rom. 1:18). This is our situation and it is our relation to God; how can we be right with him?

The answer, of course, is that we cannot be right with him; we are all wrong with him. And we all are all wrong with him because we all have sinned and come short of the glory of God. Far too frequently we fail to entertain the gravity of this fact. Hence the reality of our sin and the reality of the wrath of God upon us for our sin do not come into our reckoning. This is the reason why the grand article of justification does not ring the bells in the innermost depths of our spirit. And this is the reason why the gospel of justification is to such an extent a meaningless sound in the world and in the church of the twentieth century. We are not imbued with the profound sense of the reality of God, of his majesty and holiness. And sin, if reckoned with at all, is little more than a misfortune or maladjustment.

If we are to appreciate that which is central in the gospel, if the jubilee trumpet is to find its echo again in our hearts, our thinking must be revolutionized by the realism of the wrath of God, of the reality and gravity of our guilt, and of the divine condemnation. It is then and only then that our thinking and feeling will be rehabilitated to an understanding of God's grace in the justification of the ungodly. The question is really not so much: how can man be just with God; but how can sinful man *become* just with God? The question in this form points up the necessity of a complete reversal in our relation to God. Justification is the answer and justification is the act of God's free grace. "It is God who justifies: who is he that condemns?" (Rom. 8:33).

This truth that God justifies needs to be underlined. We do not justify ourselves. Justification is not our apology nor is it the effect in us of a process of self-excusation. It is not even our confession nor the good feeling that may be induced in us by confession. Justification is not any religious exercise in which we engage however noble and good that religious exercise may be. If we are to understand justification and appropriate its grace we must turn our thought to the action of God in justifying the ungodly. At no point is the free grace of God more manifest than in his justifying act — "being justified freely by his grace through the redemption that is in Christ Jesus" (Rom. 3:24).

The truth of justification has suffered at the hands of human perversion as much as any doctrine of Scripture. One of the ways in which it has been perverted is the failure to reckon with the meaning of the term. Justification does not mean to make righteous, or good, or holy, or upright. It is perfectly true that in the application of redemption God makes people holy and upright. He renews them after his own image. He begins to do this in regeneration and he carries it on in the work of sanctification. He will perfect it in glorification. But justification does not refer to this renewing and sanctifying grace of God. It is one of the primary errors of the Romish Church that it regards justification as the infusion of grace, as renewal and sanctification whereby we are made holy. And the seriousness of the Romish error is not so much that it has confused justification and renewal but that it has confused these two distinct acts of God's grace and eliminated from the message of the gospel the great truth of free and full justification by grace. That is why Luther endured such travail of soul as long as he was governed by Romish distortion, and the reason why he came to enjoy such exultant joy and confident assurance was that he had been emancipated from the chains by which Rome had bound him; he found the great truth that justification is something entirely different from what Rome had taught.

That justification does not mean to make holy or upright should be apparent from common use. When we justify a person we do not make that person good or upright. When a judge justifies an accused person he does not make that person an upright person. He simply declares that in his judgment the person is not guilty of the accusation but is upright in terms of the law relevant to the case. In a word, justification is simply a declaration or pronouncement respecting the relation of the person to the law which he, the judge, is required to administer. It might be, of course, that our common use would not be the same as the use of the term in Scripture. Scripture must be its own interpreter. And the question is: does Scripture usage accord with common use? This question is very easily answered. The answer is that Scripture uses the term in the same way. There are several considerations which prove this conclusion.

1. In both Testaments there are numerous passages where the term "justify" cannot mean anything else but to declare to be righteous. For example, we read, "If there be a controversy between men, and they come unto judgment, that the judges may judge them; then they shall justify the righteous, and condemn the wicked" (Deut. 25:1). It was not the function of judges to make people righteous. The meaning is simply and only that the judges were to give a just judgment and therefore they were to declare the righteous to be righteous, just as they were to declare the wicked to be wicked. Again we read, "He that justifieth the wicked, and he that condemneth the just, even they both are an abomination to the Lord" (Prov. 17:15). Now it would not be an abomination to the Lord to make the wicked upright. It would be a highly commendable thing if we could convert a wicked man and make him a righteous man. That is what God does when he regenerates a man. The meaning is more than obvious; to justify the wicked is not to make him upright but simply to declare him to be righteous when he is not. The abomination consists in giving a judgment contrary to truth and fact. Hence justification in this case is concerned only with the judgment which we give. It is declarative. In the New Testament likewise we have the same thought. "And all the people when they heard, and the publicans, justified God" (Luke 7:29). Did the people and the publicans make God upright or righteous? The thought would be blasphemous. It means that they declared God to be righteous, a perfectly proper action. They declared the righteousness of God; they vindicated him. Many other passages in both Testaments are to the same effect. But these are sufficient to show that to justify does not mean to make upright.

2. Justification is contrasted with condemnation (*cf.* Deut. 25:1; Prov. 17:15; Rom. 8:33-34). Condemn never means to make wicked, and so justify cannot mean to make good or upright.

3. There are passages in which the thought of giving judgment provides us with the sense in which we are to understand the word justification. "Who shall lay anything to the charge of God's elect? It is God that justifieth" (Rom. 8:33). The idea is not that of doing anything inwardly in the elect of God. What is in view is the accusation which an adversary may bring against the elect of God, and what is protested is that God's tribunal and judgment are ultimate. It is God's judgment that is in view when the text says, "It is God that justifieth."

Romans 8:33-34 is significant in another respect. Not only does it clearly show the meaning of the term "justify," namely, that it is judical in its import, but this passage also shows that it is this judical meaning that holds in God's justification of the ungodly. Paul is certainly using the word "justify" here in the same sense as he does earlier in the epistle. The epistle to the Romans is concerned with this very subject, the justification of sinners. That is the grand theme of the first five chapters in particular. Romans 8:33-34 conclusively shows that the meaning is that which is contrasted with the word "condemn" and that which is related to the rebuttal of a judical charge. The meaning of the word "justify," therefore, in the epistle to the Romans, and therefore in the epistle which more than any other book in Scripture unfolds the doctrine, is to declare to be righteous. Its meaning is entirely removed from the thought of making upright or holy or good or righteous.

This is what is meant when we insist that justification is forensic. It has to do with a judgment given, declared, pronounced; it is judicial or juridical or forensic. The main point of such terms is to distinguish between the kind of action which justification involves and the kind of action involved in regeneration. Regeneration is an act of God in us; justification is a judgment of God with respect to us. The distinction is like that of the distinction between the act of a surgeon and the act of a judge. The surgeon, when he removes an inward cancer, does something in us. That is not what a judge does — he gives a verdict regarding our judicial status. If we are innocent he declares accordingly.

The purity of the gospel is bound up with the recognition of this distinction. If justification is confused with regeneration or sanctification, then the door is opened for the perversion of the gospel at its center. Justification is still the article of the standing or falling church.

Justification means to declare or pronounce to be righteous. When equity is maintained such a declaration or pronouncement implies that the righteous state or standing declared to be is presupposed in the declaration. When a judge, for example, declares a person to be righteous in terms of the law which he is administering, the judge simply declares what he finds to be the case; he does not give to the person the righteous standing. This is why judges must justify the righteous and condemn the wicked (Deut. 25:1). Justification in such a case merely takes account of the character and conduct of the person concerned and the judge gives his verdict accordingly. He justifies those who are righteous. The declaration of the fact presupposes the fact which is declared to be.

The justification with which we are now concerned, however, is God's justification of the ungodly. It is not the justification of persons who are righteous but of persons who are wicked and, therefore, of persons who are under God's condemnation and curse. How can this be? God's judgment is always according to truth; it is not only one of equity but one of perfect equity. How then can he justify those who are unrighteous and totally unrighteous at that?

We are here faced with something completely unique. It cannot be denied that God justifies the ungodly (Rom. 4:5; *cf.* Rom. 3:19-24). If man were to do this it would be an abomination in God's sight. Man must *condemn* the wicked, and he may *justify* only the righteous. God justifies the wicked and he does what no man may do. Yet God is not unrighteous. He is just when he justifies the ungodly (Rom. 3:26). What is it that enables him to be just when he justifies sinners?

It is here that the mere notion of declaring to be righteous is seen to be inadequate of itself to express the fullness of what is involved in God's justification of the ungodly. Much more is entailed than our English expression "declare to be righteous" denotes. In God's justification of sinners there is a totally new factor which does not hold in any other case of justification. And this new factor arises from the totally different situation which God's justification of sinners contemplates and from the marvellous provisions of God's grace and justice to meet that situation. God does what none other could do and he does here what he does nowhere else. What is this unique and incomparable thing?

In God's justification of sinners there is no deviation from the rule that what is declared to be is presupposed to be. God's judgment is according to truth here as elsewhere. The peculiarity of God's action consists in this that he causes to be the righteous state or relation which is declared to be. We must remember that justification is always forensic or judicial. Therefore what God does in this case is that he constitutes the new and righteous judicial relation as well as declares this new relation to be. He constitutes the ungodly righteous, and consequently can declare them to be righteous. In the justification of sinners there is a constitutive act as well as a declarative. Or, if we will, we may say that the declarative act of God in the justification of the ungodly is constitutive. In this consists its incomparable character.

This conclusion that justification is constitutive is not only an inference drawn from the considerations of God's truth and equity; it is expressly stated in the Scripture itself. It is with the subject of justification that Paul is dealing when he says, "For as through the disobedience of the one man the many were constituted sinners, even so through the obedience of the one the many will be constituted righteous" (Rom. 5:19). The parallel expressions which Paul uses in this chapter are to the same effect. In Romans 5:17 he speaks of those who receive "the free gift of righteousness" and in verse 18 of the judgment which passes upon men unto justification of life "through one righteousness." It is clear that the justification which is unto eternal life Paul regards as consisting in our being constituted righteous, in our receiving righteousness as a free gift, and this righteousness is none other than the righteousness of the one man Jesus Christ; it is the righteousness of his obedience. Hence grace reigns through righteousness unto eternal life through Jesus Christ our Lord (Rom. 5:21). This is the truth which has been expressed as the imputation to us of the righteousness of Christ. Justification is therefore a constitutive act whereby the righteousness of Christ is imputed to our account and we are accordingly accepted as righteous in God's sight. When we think of such an act of grace on God's part, we have the answer to our question: how can God justify the ungodly? The righteousness of Christ is the righteousness of his perfect obedience, a righteousness undefiled and undefilable, a righteousness which not only warrants the justification of the ungodly but one that necessarily elicits and constrains such justification. God cannot but accept into his favor those who are invested with the righteousness of his own Son. While his wrath is revealed from heaven against all unrighteousness and ungodliness of men, his good pleasure is also revealed from heaven upon the righteousness of his well-beloved and only-begotten.

Those justified may well exult in the words of the prophet, "Surely, shall one say, in the Lord have I righteousness and strength.... In the Lord shall all the seed of Israel be justified, and shall glory" (Isa. 45:24-25). "I will greatly rejoice in the Lord, my soul shall be joyful in my God; for he hath clothed me with the garments of salvation, he hath covered me with the robe of righteousness, as a bridegroom decketh himself with ornaments, and as a bride adorneth herself with her jewels" (Isa. 61:10). "No weapon that is formed against thee shall prosper; and every tongue that shall rise against thee in judgment thou shalt condemn. This is the heritage of the servants of the Lord, and their righteousness is of me, saith the Lord" (Isa. 54:17). And the protestation of the apostle becomes more meaningful: "Who shall lay anything to the charge of God's elect? It is God that justifieth" (Rom. 8:33).

Justification is both a declarative and a constitutive act of God's free grace. It is constitutive in order that it may be truly declarative. God must constitute the new relationship as well as declare it to be. The constitutive act consists in the imputation to us of the obedience and righteousness of Christ. The obedience of Christ must therefore be regarded as the ground of justification; it is the righteousness which God not only takes into account but reckons to our account when he justifies the ungodly. This doctrine, however, needs further examination if the biblical basis for it is to be made more apparent.

In Genesis 15:6 it is said of Abraham that he believed in the Lord and he reckoned it to him for righteousness. This text is quoted repeatedly in the New Testament (Rom. 4:3, 9, 22; Gal. 3:6; James 2:23) and it might appear that it was the faith of Abraham which was reckoned as the righteousness on the basis of which he was justified, that faith itself was accepted by God as fulfilling the requirements necessary for a full and perfect justification. If this were the case then Abraham was justified and all other believers also are justified on the ground of faith and because of faith. It is important to observe in this connection that the Scripture never uses such terms. It speaks always of our being justified *by* faith, or *through* faith, or *upon* faith, but never speaks of our being justified *on account of* faith or *because* of faith. If, however, we are justified on the basis of faith the expression that would most accurately express such a thought would be that we are justified on account of faith. The fact that Scripture, and especially the apostle Paul, refrains from such terms is itself sufficient to make us careful not to think or speak in any way which would suggest such a view of justification. But there are also numerous other considerations which show that faith is not itself the righteousness, as they also show that the righteousness of justification is not anything wrought in us or done by us. There are several arguments which may be set forth.

I. A righteousness wrought in us, even though it were perfect and eliminated all future sin, would not measure up to the requirements of the full and irrevocable justification which the Scripture represents justification to be. Such a righteousness would not obliterate the sin and unrighteousness of the past and the condemnation resting upon us for our past sin. But justification includes the remission of all sin and condemnation. Consequently the righteousness which is the basis of such justification must be one that will take care of past sin as well as provide for the future. Inwrought righteousness does not measure up to this need. And we must also bear in mind that the righteousness wrought in us by regeneration and sanctification is never in this life perfect. Hence it cannot in any sense measure up to the kind of righteousness required. Only a perfect righteousness can provide the basis for a complete, perfect, and irreversible justification. Furthermore, justification gives a title to and secures eternal life (Rom. 5:17-18, 21). A righteousness wrought in us equips for the enjoyment of eternal life but it cannot be the ground of such a reward.

2. Justification is not by the righteousness of performance on our part; it is not of works (Rom. 3:20; 4:2; 10:3-4; Gal. 2:16; 3:11; 5:4; Phil. 3:9). The Scripture is so insistent upon this that it is only by spiritual blindness and distortion of the most aggravated type that justification by works could ever be entertained or proposed in any form or to any degree. The Romish doctrine bears the patent hall-marks of such distortion.

3. We are justified by grace. It is not the reward of anything in us or wrought by us but proceeds from God's free and unmerited favor (Rom. 3:24ff.; 5:15-21).

We thus see that if we are to find the righteousness which supplies the basis of the full and perfect justification which God bestows upon the ungodly we cannot find it in anything that resides in us, nor in anything which God does in us, nor in anything which we do. We must look away from ourselves to something which is of an entirely different sort in an entirely different direction. What is the direction which the Scripture indicates?

1. It is in Christ we are justified (Acts 13:39; Rom. 8:1; 1 Cor. 6:11; Gal. 2:17). At the outset we are here advised that it is by union with Christ and by some specific relation to him involved in that union that we are justified.

2. It is through Christ's sacrificial and redemptive work (Rom. 3:24; 5:9; 8:33-34). We are justified in Jesus' blood. The particular significance of this truth in this connection is that it is the once-for-all redemptive accomplishment of Christ that is brought into the center of attention when we are thinking of justification. It is therefore something objective to ourselves and not the work of God's grace in our hearts and minds and lives.

3. It is by the righteousness of God that we are justified

(Rom. 1:17; 3:21, 22; 10:3; Phil. 3:9). In other words, the righteousness of our justification is a God-righteousness. Nothing more conclusively demonstrates that it is not a righteousness which is ours. Righteousness wrought in us or wrought by us, even though it be altogether of the grace of God and even though it be perfect in character, is not a God-righteousness. It is, after all, a human righteousness. But the commanding insistence of the Scripture is that in justification it is the righteousness of God which is revealed from faith to faith, and therefore a righteousness which is contrasted not only with human unrighteousness but with human righteousness. It is righteousness which is *divine* in quality. It is not, of course, the divine attribute of justice or righteousness, but, nevertheless, it is a righteousness with divine attributes or qualities and therefore a righteousness which is of divine property.

4. The righteousness of justification is the righteousness and obedience of Christ (Rom. 5:17-19). Here we have the final consideration which confirms all of the foregoing considerations and sets them in clear focus. This is the final reason why we are pointed away from ourselves to Christ and his accomplished work. And this is the reason why the righteousness of justification is the righteousness of God. It is the righteousness of Christ wrought by him in human nature, the righteousness of his obedience unto death, even the death of the cross. But, as such, it is the righteousness of the God-man, a righteousness which measures up to the requirements of our sinful and sin-cursed situation, a righteousness which meets all the demands of a complete and irrevocable justification, and a righteousness fulfilling all these demands because it is a righteousness of divine property and character, a righteousness undefiled and inviolable. Grace reigns *through righteousness* unto eternal life through Jesus Christ our Lord (Rom. 5:21). "Blessed is the people that know the joyful sound: they shall walk, O Lord, in the light

of thy countenance. In thy name shall they rejoice all the day: and in thy righteousness shall they be exalted" (Ps. 89:15-16).

Justification is an act which proceeds from God's free grace. It is an act of God and of God alone. And the righteousness which supplies its ground or basis is the righteousness of God. It might seem that this emphasis upon divine action would not only make it inappropriate but inconsistent for any activity of which we are the agents to be given any instrumentality or efficiency in connection with justification. But the Scripture makes it quite clear that activity on the part of the recipient is given its own place in relation to this act of God's grace. The activity on the part of the recipient is that of faith, and it is faith alone that is brought into this relationship to justification. We are justified by faith, or through faith, or upon faith (cf. Rom. 1:17; 3:22, 25-28, 30; 4:3, 5, 16, 24; 5:1; Gal. 2:16; 3:8, 9; 5:1-5; Phil 3:9)

There have been good protestants who have maintained that this faith is not the antecedent of justification, but the consequent, that we do not believe in order to be justified but we believe because we have been justified, and that the faith referred to is the faith that we have been justified. The witness of Scripture does not appear to bear out this view of the relation of faith to justification. It is true, of course, that there is a faith which is consequent to justification. We cannot believe that we have been justified until we are first justified. But there is good reason for insisting that this reflex or secondary act of faith is not the faith in view when we are said to be justified by faith and that this faith by which we are justified is the initial and primary act of faith in Jesus Christ by which in our effectual calling we are united to Christ and invested with his righteousness unto our acceptance with God and justification by him.

There are several considerations which favor this view of the Scripture teaching. I shall mention only two.

1. It appears quite unnatural and forced to regard the sustained emphasis of the Scripture that we are justified by faith in any other way. When the Scripture speaks of justification in these cases, it does not refer to our consciousness or assurance of justification, but to the divine act by which we are actually justified. Justification does not consist in that which is reflected in our consciousness; it consists in the divine act of acquittal and acceptance. And it is precisely this that is said to be by faith.

2. There is one passage in Paul which is quite illumining, in this respect. It is Galatians 2:16. "Knowing that a man is not justified by the works of the law, but by the faith of Jesus Christ, even we have believed in Jesus Christ, that we might be justified by the faith of Christ, and not by the works of the law." Paul here says that we have believed in Jesus Christ in order that we might be justified by the faith of Christ. In a word, faith in Christ is in order to justification, and is therefore regarded as antecedent to it (cf. also Rom. 4:23-24).

We may conclude that the Scripture means to teach that the justifying act of God supervenes upon the act of faith, that God justifies those who believe in Jesus and upon the event of faith. But faith, we must remember, is an act or exercise on the part of men. It is not God who believes in Jesus Christ, but the sinner who is being justified. Therefore faith is an indispensable instrumentality in connection with justification. We are justified by faith and faith is the prerequisite. And only faith is brought into relation to justification. Why is this the case?

It could be sufficient for us to know that in the divine appointment it is so. Oftentimes in the revelation of the counsel of God this is all we can say and it is all we need to say. But in this case we can with good warrant say more. There are apparent reasons why justification is by faith and by faith alone. First, it is altogether consonant with the fact that it is by grace. "Therefore it is of faith, in order that it might be according to grace" (Rom. 4:16). Faith and grace are wholly complementary. Second, faith is entirely congruous with the fact that the ground of justification is the righteousness of Christ. The specific quality of faith is that it receives and rests upon another, in this case Christ and his righteousness. No other grace, however important it may be in connection with salvation as a whole, has this as its specific and distinguishing quality. We are justified therefore by faith. Third, justification by faith and faith alone exemplifies the freeness and richness of the gospel of grace. If we were to be justified by works, in any degree or to any extent, then there would be no gospel at all. For what works of righteousness can a condemned, guilty, and depraved sinner offer to God? That we are justified by faith advertises the grand article of the gospel of grace that we are not justified by works of law. Faith stands in antithesis to works; there can be no amalgam of these two (cf. Gal. 5:4). That we are justified by faith is what engenders hope in a convicted sinner's heart. He knows he has nothing to offer. And this truth assures him that he needs nothing to offer, yea, it assures him that it is an abomination to God to presume to offer. We are justified by faith and therefore simply by entrustment of ourselves, in all our dismal hopelessness, to the Savior whose righteousness is undefiled and undefilable. Justification by faith alone lies at the heart of the gospel and it is the article that makes the lame man leap as an hart and the tongue of the dumb sing. Justification is that by which grace reigns through righteousness unto eternal life; it is for the believer alone and it is for the believer by faith alone. It is the righteousness of God from faith to faith (Rom. 1:17; cf. 3:22).

It is an old and time-worn objection that this doctrine ministers to licence and looseness. Only those who know not the power of the gospel will plead such misconception. Justification is by faith alone, but not by a faith that is alone. Justification is not all that is embraced in the gospel of redeeming grace. Christ is a complete Savior and it is not justification alone that the believing sinner possesses in him. And faith is not the only response in the heart of him who has entrusted himself to Christ for salvation. Faith alone justifies but a justified person with faith alone would be a monstrosity which never exists in the kingdom of grace. Faith works itself out through love (cf. Gal. 5:6). And faith without works is dead (cf. James 2:17-20), It is living faith that justifies and living faith unites to Christ both in the virtue of his death and in the power of his resurrection. No one has entrusted himself to Christ for deliverance from the guilt of sin who has not also entrusted himself to him for deliverance from the power of sin. "What shall we say then? Shall we continue in sin, that grace may abound? God forbid. How shall we, that are dead to sin, live any longer therein?" (Rom. 6:1-2).

CHAPTER VI

Adoption

Adoption is an act of God's grace distinct from and additional to the other acts of grace involved in the application of redemption. It might seem quite unnecessary to say this. Does not the term itself and the specific meaning which attaches to it clearly imply its distinctiveness? Yet it is not superfluous to emphasize the fact that it is a distinct act carrying with it its own peculiar privileges. It is particularly important to remember that it is not the same as justification or regeneration. Too frequently it has been regarded as simply an aspect of justification or as another way of stating the privilege conferred by regeneration. It is much more than either or both of these acts of grace.

Justification means our acceptance with God as righteous and the bestowal of the title to everlasting life. Regeneration is the renewing of our hearts after the image of God. But these blessings in themselves, however precious they are, do not indicate what is conferred by the act of adoption. By adoption the redeemed become sons and daughters of the Lord God Almighty; they are introduced into and given the privileges of God's family. Neither justification nor regeneration expresses precisely that. A text which sets forth the special character of adoption is John 1:12: "But as many as received him, to them gave he right (authority) to become children of God, to those who believe on his name." We be-come children of God by the bestowment of a right or by the conferring of authority, and this is given to them who believe on Jesus' name.

There are a few things to be said, however, about the relation of adoption to these other acts of grace. 1. Though adoption is distinct it is never separable from justification and regeneration. The person who is justified is always the recipient of sonship. And those who are given the right to be-come sons of God are those who, as John 1:13 indicates, "were born not of blood nor of the will of the flesh nor of the will of man but of God." 2. Adoption is, like justification, a judicial act. In other words, it is the bestowal of a status, or standing, not the generating within us of a new nature or character. It concerns a relationship and not the attitude or disposition which enables us to recognize and cultivate that relationship. 3. Those adopted into God's family are also given the Spirit of adoption whereby they are able to recognize their sonship and exercise the privileges which go with it. "And because ye are sons, God hath sent forth the Spirit of his Son into our hearts, crying Abba Father" (Gal. 4:6; cf. Rom. 8:15-16). The Spirit of adoption is the consequence but this does not itself constitute adoption. 4. There is a close relationship between adoption and regeneration. So close is this connection that some would say that we are sons of God both by participa-tion of nature and by deed of adoption. There is Scripture evidence which might support this inference. There are two ways whereby we may becomes members of a human fam-ily — we may be born into it or we may be adopted into it. The former is by natural generation, the latter is by legal act. It may be that the Scripture represents us as entering into the family of God by both — by generation and by adoption. However, this does not appear to be conclusive. In any case, there is a very close interdependence between the generative act of God's grace (regeneration) and the adoptive. When God adopts men and women into his family he insures that not only may they have the rights and privileges of his sons and daughters but also the nature or disposition consonant with such a status. This he does by regeneration — he renews them after his image in knowledge, righteousness, and holiness. God never has in his family those who are alien to its atmosphere and spirit and station. Regeneration is the prerequisite of adoption. It is the same Holy Spirit who regenerates who is also sent into the hearts of the adopted, crying Abba Father. But adoption itself is not simply regeneration, nor is it the Spirit of adoption — the one is prerequisite, the other is consequent.

Adoption, as the term clearly implies, is an act of transfer from an alien family into the family of God himself. This is surely the apex of grace and privilege. We would not dare to conceive of such grace far less to claim it apart from God's own revelation and assurance. It staggers imagination because of its amazing condescension and love. The Spirit alone could be the seal of it in our hearts. "Eye hath not seen, nor ear heard, neither have entered into the heart of man, the things which God hath prepared for them that love him. But God hath revealed them unto us by his Spirit: for the Spirit searcheth all things, yea, the deep things of God" (1 Cor. 2:9-10). It is only as there is the conjunction of the witness of revelation and the inward witness of the Spirit in our hearts that we are able to scale this pinnacle of faith and say with filial confidence and love, Abba Father.

Adoption is concerned with the fatherhood of God in relation to men. When we think of God's fatherhood it is necessary to make certain distinctions. There is, first of all, God's fatherhood which is exclusively trinitarian, the fatherhood of the Father, the first person of the trinity, in relation to the Son, the second person. This applies only to God the Father in his eternal and necessary relation to the Son and to the Son alone. It is unique and exclusive. No one else, not even the Holy Spirit, is the Son in this sense. It does not apply to angels or men. In modern theology it is sometimes said that men by adoption come to share in Christ's Sonship and thus enter into the divine life of the trinity. This is grave confusion and error. The eternal Son of God is the only-begotten and no one shares in his Sonship, just as God the Father is not the Father of any other in the sense in which he is the Father of the only-begotten and eternal Son.

In relation to men there is what has sometimes been called the universal fatherhood of God. It is true that there is a sense in which God may be said to be the Father of all men. Creatively and providentially he gives to all men life and breath and all things. In him all live and move and have their being. It is this relation that is referred to in such passages as Acts 17:25-29; Hebrews 12:9; James 1:18. Since we are the offspring of God, since he is the Father of spirits and the Father of lights it may be scriptural to speak of this relation which God sustains to all men in creation and providence as one of fatherhood and therefore of universal fatherhood. There are other passages in Scripture which might appear to speak even more explicitly of this relation in terms of father but when examined carefully some of them can clearly be shown not to refer to this fatherhood and others more probably refer to a much more specific and restricted fatherhood. In Malachi 2:10, for example, "Have we not all one father? hath not one God created us?", it is not by any means certain that the allusion is to original creation and to God as Father of all men in virtue of creation. What needs in any case to be noted is that on relatively few occasions in Scripture is the relation which God sustains to men in virtue of creation and general providence spoken of in terms of God's fatherhood. The term "Father" as applied to God and the title "son of God" as applied to men are all but uniformly in Scripture reserved for that particular relationship that is constituted by redemption and adoption. This teaches us the lesson that the great message of Scripture respecting the fatherhood of God, the message epitomized in such a text as, "ye have not received the spirit of bondage again to fear, but ye have received the Spirit of adoption, whereby we cry Abba Father" (Rom. 8:15) or in the prayer which Jesus taught his disciples to pray, "Our Father who art in heaven" (Matt. 6:9), is not that of the universal fatherhood of God but the message of that most specific and intimate relationship which God constitutes with those who believe in Jesus' name. To substitute the message of God's universal fatherhood for that which is constituted by redemption and adoption is to annul the gospel; it means the degradation of this highest and richest of relationships to the level of that relationship which all men sustain to God by creation. In a word, it is to deprive the gospel of its redemptive meaning. And it encourages men in the delusion that our creaturehood is the guarantee of our adoption into God's family.

The great truth of God's fatherhood and of the sonship which God bestows upon men is one that belongs to the application of redemption. It is true in respect of all men no more than are effectual calling, regeneration, and justification. God becomes the Father of his own people by the act of adoption. It is the marvel of such grace that constrained the apostle John to exclaim, "Behold what manner of love the Father hath bestowed upon us that we should be called children of God" (1 John 3:1). And to assure his readers of this privilege as a present possession and not simply a hope for the future he adds immediately, "and we are." To indicate the cleavage which this status institutes among men he continues, "On this account the world does not know us, because it did not know him." Lest there should be any doubt regarding the reality of the sonship bestowed he insists, "Beloved, now are we the children of God" (ver. 2). John had pondered and learned well the words of the Lord himself when he said, "He that loveth me shall be loved of my Father.... If a man love me he will keep my words: and my Father will love him, and we will come unto him, and make our abode with him" (John 14:21, 23). And now in writing his first epistle his heart overflows with wonderment at this donation of the Father's love, "Behold what manner of love the Father hath bestowed on us." It is specifically the Father's act of grace. John could not get over it and he never will. Eternity will not exhaust its marvel.

God becomes the Father of his own people by the act of adoption. It is specifically God the Father who is the agent of this act of grace. "Behold what manner of love the Father hath bestowed upon us that we should be called children of God, and we are" (1 John 3:1). The question arises: who is to be regarded as the Father of those who are adopted into God's family? Is it God viewed as the three persons of the trinity or is it specifically God the Father? And when the people of God address God as Father, whom are they addressing? Is it the Godhead, Father, Son, and Holy Spirit, or is it the Father, the first person of the Godhead? It is to this question that we must now turn our attention.

There are several considerations drawn from the Scripture which indicate that it is God the Father who is Father and that by adoption the people of God become sons of the first person of the trinity. At least the Scripture would indicate that when the Fatherhood of God in relation to men is contemplated it is the Father *specifically* who comes into this relation to them.

1. The title "Father" is the distinguishing name of the first person of the trinity. This title belongs to him, first of all, because in the relations of the persons of the Godhead to one another he alone is Father, just as the second person alone is

Son and the third person alone is Holy Spirit. When our Lord spoke of the Father and addressed the Father it was always the first person of the trinity whom he had in view. It is the first person alone who is the God and Father of our Lord Jesus Christ.

2. In John 20:17 we have a very instructive word of our Lord. There Jesus is reported by John as having said to Mary Magdalene, "Touch me not, for I am not yet ascended unto the Father: but go to my brethren and say unto them, I ascend unto my Father and your Father and my God and your God." It is clear that when Jesus said, "I am not yet ascended unto the Father" he could mean none other than the first person of the trinity, the Father. Again when he continued, "I ascend unto my Father" he meant none other than the first person because only the Father could Jesus call "my Father." But the important observation for our present purpose is that the same person whom Jesus calls "my Father" he also calls the Father of the disciples; the Father to whom Jesus was about to ascend is not only his Father but also the Father of the disciples. It is the same person of the Father, though the distinctness of the relationship to the Father is jealously guarded by our Lord. He does not say "I ascend to our Father" but rather "I ascend to my Father and your Father and my God and your God."

3. Jesus very frequently calls the Father, the first person of the trinity, "my Father who is in heaven." The form of expression slightly varies but it is always to the same effect. And he also in speaking to his disciples uses the same kind of expression, "your Father who is in heaven." When Jesus speaks of his own Father in heaven he can refer to none other than the Father. Hence the similiarity of expression in the title, "your Father who is in heaven" would lead us to the conclusion that the same person is in view and that it is the Father who is regarded as the Father of the disciples.

145

4. In the New Testament in general the title, "the Father" is undoubtedly the personal name of the first person of the trinity. In the epistles of Paul quite frequently the title, "God" is also the personal name of the first person in distinction from the Son and the Spirit. In several passages, also, the first person is called "the God and Father of our Lord Jesus Christ" (Rom. 15:6; 2 Cor. 1:3; 11:31; Eph. 1:3; Col. 1:3; 1 Pet. 1:3). There can be no question but this is the Father in distinction from the Son and the Spirit. The same is true of the title, "God the Father" or its close equivalent (Gal. 1:1; Eph. 6:23; Phil. 2:11; 1 Thess. 1:1; 2 Thess. 1:2; 1 Tim. 1:2; 2 Tim. 1:2; Titus 1:4; 1 Pet. 1:2; 2 Pet. 1:17; 2 John 3; Jude 1; Rev. 1:6). In nearly all these passages God the Father is distinguished from the Son and in 1 Peter 1:2 from the Holy Spirit. Now the important observation for our present interest is that when God is called the Father of believers we have close similarity of expression to that which we find in these cases just cited where there can be no question that the person of the trinity in view is the Father, the first person. In Romans 1:7 we have the salutation, "Grace to you and peace from God our Father and the Lord Jesus Christ" (see also 1 Cor. 1:3; 2 Cor. 1:2; Gal. 1:3; Eph. 1:2; Phil. 1:2; Philem. 3; cf. Gal. 1:4; Phil. 4:20; Col. 1:2; 1 Thess. 1:3; 3:11, 13; 2 Thess. 1:1-2). In such passages as these not only is there the similarity of expression to the titles, "God the Father" and "the God and Father of our Lord Jesus Christ" but also the person denominated "God our Father" is distinguished from "the Lord Jesus Christ." And this means simply that the person who is called "our Father" is distinct from the Lord Jesus Christ. This is equivalent to saying that it is the Father who is *our* Father. In this same connection 2 Thessalonians 2:16 illustrates well the distinctness of the first person as the person in view in the fatherly relation which God sustains to men. "But our Lord Jesus Christ himself and God our Father, who loved us and gave us everlasting consolation and good

hope through grace, comfort your hearts and establish them in every good work and word."

On the basis of this evidence we are led to the conclusion that when God is thought of in terms of adoption as "our heavenly Father" or "our Father" it is the first person of the trinity, the person who is specifically the Father, who is in view. The people of God are the sons of God the Father and he sustains to them this highest and most intimate of relationships. This fact enhances the marvel of the relationship established by adoption. The first person of the Godhead is not only the God and Father of our Lord Jesus Christ but is also the God and Father of those who believe in Jesus' name. The relation of God as Father to the Son must not be equated, of course, with the relation of God as Father to men. Eternal generation must not be equated with adoption. Our Lord himself guarded the distinction. He did not include the disciples with himself and in community with them call the Father "our Father." He said to his disciples, "After this manner therefore pray ye: Our Father who art in heaven" (Matt. 6:9). He did not, and as a matter of fact could not, pray with them the prayer he taught them to pray. And he said to Mary Magdalene, "I ascend unto my Father and your Father and my God and your God" (John 20:17). But though the relation of Fatherhood differs, it is the same person who is the Father of the Lord Jesus Christ in the ineffable mystery of the trinity who is the Father of believers in the mystery of his adoptive grace. God the Father is not only the specific agent in the act of adoption; he also constitutes those who believe in Jesus' name his own children. Could anything disclose the marvel of adoption or certify the security of its tenure and privelege more effectively than the fact that the Father himself, on account of whom are all things and through whom are all things, who made the captain of salvation perfect through sufferings, becomes by deed of grace the Father of the many sons whom he will bring to glory? And that is the reason why the captain of salvation himself is not ashamed to call them brethren and can exult with joy unspeakable, "Behold I and the children whom God hath given to me" (Heb. 2:13).

CHAPTER VII

Sanctification

The Presuppositions

Sanctification is an aspect of the application of redemption. In the application of redemption there is order, and the order is one of progression until it reaches its consummation in the liberty of the glory of the children of God (Rom. 8:21, 30). Sanctification is not the first step in the application of redemption; it presupposes other steps such as effectual calling, regeneration, justification, and adoption. All of these bear intimately upon sanctification. The two anterior steps or aspects which are particularly relevant to sanctification are calling and regeneration. Sanctification is a work of God *in us*, and calling and regeneration are acts of God which have their immediate effects *in us*. Calling is addressed to our consciousness and elicits response in our consciousness. Regeneration is renewal which registers itself in our consciousness in the exercises of faith and repentance, love and obedience. There are also other considerations which show the particular relevance of calling and regeneration to the process of sanctification. It is by calling that we are united to Christ, and it is this union with Christ which binds the people of God to the efficacy and virtue by which they are sanctified. Regeneration is wrought by the Holy Spirit (John 3:3, 5, 6, 8) and by this act the people of God become indwelt by the Holy Spirit; they become in New Testament terms "Spiritual." Sanctification is specifically the work of this indwelling and directing Holy Spirit.

An all-important consideration derived from the priority of calling and regeneration is that sin is dethroned in every person who is effectually called and regenerated. Calling unites to Christ (1 Cor. 1:9), and if the person called is united to Christ he is united to him in the virtue of his death and the power of his resurrection; he is dead to sin, the old man has been crucified, the body of sin has been destroyed, sin does not have the dominion (Rom. 6:2-6, 14). In Romans 6:14, Paul is not simply giving an exhortation. He is making an apodictic statement to the effect that sin will not have dominion over the person who is under grace. He gives exhortation in very similar language in the context, but here he is making an emphatic negation — "sin will not have dominion." If we view the question from the standpoint of regeneration we reach the same conclusion. The Holy Spirit is the controlling and directing agent in every regenerate person. Hence the fundamental principle, the governing disposition, the prevailing character of every regenerate person is holiness — he is "Spiritual" and he delights in the law of the Lord after the inward man (1 Cor. 2:14-15; Rom. 7:22). This must be the sense in which John speaks of the regenerate person as not doing sin and as unable to sin (1 John 3:9, 5:18). It is not that he is sinless (cf. 1 John 1:8; 2:1). What John is stressing is surely the fact that the regenerate person cannot commit the sin that is unto death (1 John 5:16), he cannot deny that Jesus is the Son of God and has come in the flesh (1 John 4:1-4), he cannot abandon himself again to iniquity, he keeps himself and the evil one does not touch him. Greater is he who is in the believer than he who is in the world (1 John 4:4).

We must appreciate this teaching of Scripture. Every one called effectually by God and regenerated by the Spirit has secured the victory in the terms of Romans 6:14; 1 John 3:9; 5:4, 18. And this victory is actual or it is nothing. It is a reflection upon and a deflection from the pervasive New Testament witness to speak of it as merely potential or positional. It is actual and practical as much as anything comprised in the application of redemption is actual and practical.

Respecting this freedom from the dominion of sin, this victory over the power of sin, it is likewise to be recognized that it is not achieved by a process, nor by our striving or working to that end. It is achieved once for all by union with Christ and the regenerating grace of the Holy Spirit. Perfectionists are right when they insist that this victory is not achieved by us nor by working or striving or laboring; they are correct in maintaining that it is a momentary act realized by faith. But they also make three radical mistakes, mistakes which distort their whole construction of sanctification.

(1) They fail to recognize that this victory is the possession of every one who is born again and effectually called. (2) They construe the victory as a blessing separable from the state of justification. (3) They represent it as something very different from what the Scripture represents it to be — they portray it as freedom from sinning or freedom from conscious sin. It is wrong to use these texts to support any other view of the victory entailed than that which the Scripture teaches it to be, namely, the radical breach with the power and love of sin which is necessarily the possession of every one who has been united to Christ. Union with Christ is union with him in the efficacy of his death and in the virtue of his resurrection — he who thus died and rose again with Christ is freed from sin, and sin will not exercise the dominion.

The Concern of Sanctification

This deliverance from the power of sin secured by union with Christ and from the defilement of sin secured by regeneration does not eliminate all sin from the heart and life of the believer. There is still indwelling sin (cf. Rom. 6:20; 7:14-25; 1 John 1:8; 2:1). The believer is not yet so conformed to the image of Christ that he is holy, harmless, undefiled, and separate from sinners. Sanctification is concerned precisely with this fact and it has as its aim the elimination of all sin and complete conformation to the image of God's own Son, to be holy as the Lord is holy. If we take the concept of entire sanctification seriously we are shut up to the conclusion that it will not be realized until the body of our humiliation will be transformed into the likeness of the body of Christ's glory, when the corruptible will put on incorruption and the mortal will put on immortality (Phil. 3:21; 1 Cor. 15:54).

We must appreciate the gravity of that with which sanctification is concerned. There are several respects in which this must be viewed.

(1) All sin in the believer is the contradiction of God's holiness. Sin does not change its character as sin because the person in whom it dwells and by whom it is committed is a believer. It is true that the believer sustains a new relation to God. There is no judicial condemnation for him and the judicial wrath of God does not rest upon him (Rom. 8:1). God is his Father and he is God's son. The Holy Spirit dwells in him and is his advocate. Christ is the believer's advocate with the Father. But the sin which resides in the believer and which he commits is of such a character that it deserves the wrath of God and the fatherly displeasure of God is evoked by this sin. Remaining, indwelling sin is therefore the contradiction of all that he is as a regenerate person and son of God. It is the contradiction of God himself, after whose image he has

been recreated. We feel the tremor of the apostle's solicitude when he says, "My little children, these things write I unto you in order that ye sin not" (1 John 2:1). Lest there should be any disposition to take sin for granted, to be content with the *status quo*, to indulge sin or turn the grace of God into lasciviousness, John is jealous to summon believers to the remembrance that everyone who has hope in God "purifies himself even as he is pure" (1 John 3:3) and that all that is in the world, "the lust of the flesh, the lust of the eyes, and the pride of life, is not of the Father but is of the world" (1 John 2:16).

(2) The presence of sin in the believer involves conflict in his heart and life. If there is remaining, indwelling sin, there must be the conflict which Paul describes in Romans 7:14ff. It is futile to argue that this conflict is not normal. If there is still sin to any degree in one who is indwelt by the Holy Spirit, then there is tension, yes, contradiction, within the heart of that person. Indeed, the more sanctified the person is, the more conformed he is to the image of his Savior, the more he must recoil against every lack of conformity to the holiness of God. The deeper his apprehension of the majesty of God, the greater the intensity of his love to God, the more persistent his yearning for the attainment of the prize of the high calling of God in Christ Jesus, the more conscious will he be of the gravity of the sin which remains and the more poignant will be his detestation of it. The more closely he comes to the holiest of all, the more he apprehends the sinfulness that is his and he must cry out, "O wretched man that I am" (Rom. 7:24). Was this not the effect in all the people of God as they came into closer proximity to the revelation of God's holiness? "Woe is me! for I am undone, because I am a man of unclean lips, and I dwell in the midst of a people of unclean lips; for mine eyes have seen the King, the Lord of hosts" (Isa. 6:5). "I have heard of thee by the hearing of the ear; but now mine eye seeth thee. Wherefore I abhor myself, and

repent in dust and ashes" (Job 42:5-6). Truly biblical sanctification has no affinity with the self-complacency which, ig-
nores or fails to take into account the sinfulness of every lack
of conformity to the image of him who was holy, harmless,
and undefiled. "Ye shall be perfect therefore as your heavenly
Father is perfect" (Matt. 5:48).

(3) There must be a constant and increasing appreciation
that though sin still remains it does not have the mastery.
There is a total difference between surviving sin and reigning
sin, the regenerate in conflict with sin and the unregenerate
complacent to sin. It is one thing for sin to live in us: it is another for us to live in sin. It is one thing for the enemy to occupy the capital; it is another for his defeated hosts to harass
the garrisons of the kingdom. It is of paramount concern for
the Christian and for the interests of his sanctification that
he should know that sin does not have the dominion over
him, that the forces of redeeming, regenerative, and sanctifying grace have been brought to bear upon him in that
which is central in his moral and spiritual being, that he is
the habitation of God through the Spirit, and that Christ has
been formed in him the hope of glory. This is equivalent to
saying that he must reckon himself to be dead indeed unto
sin but alive unto God through Jesus Christ his Lord. It is the
faith of this fact that provides the basis for, and the incentive
to the fulfillment of, the exhortation, "Let not sin therefore
reign in your mortal body to the end that ye should obey
its lusts, neither present ye your members as instruments
of unrighteousness to sin, but present yourselves to God as
those alive from the dead and your members as instruments
of righteousness to God" (Rom. 6:12-13). In this matter the
indicative lies at the basis of the imperative and our faith of
fact is indispensable to the discharge of duty. The faith that
sin will not have the dominion is the dynamic in bondservice
to righteousness and to God so that we may have the fruit

unto holiness and the end everlasting life (Rom. 6:17, 22). It is the concern of sanctification that sin be more and more mortified and holiness ingenerated and cultivated.

The Agent of Sanctification

It is necessary to be reminded that in the last analysis we do not sanctify ourselves. It is God who sanctifies (1 Thess. 5:23). Specifically it is the Holy Spirit who is the agent of sanctification. In this connection certain observations require to be made.

(1) The mode of the Spirit's operation in sanctification is encompassed with mystery. We do not know the mode of the Spirit's indwelling nor the mode of his efficient working in the hearts and minds and wills of God's people by which they are progressively cleansed from the defilement of sin and more and more transfigured after the image of Christ. While we must not do prejudice to the fact that the Spirit's work in our hearts reflects itself in our awareness and consciousness, while we must not relegate sanctification to the realm of the subconscious and fail to recognize that sanctification draws within its orbit the whole field of conscious activity on our part, yet we must also appreciate the fact that there is an agency on the part of the Holy Spirit that far surpasses analysis or introspection on our part. The effects of this constant and uninterrupted agency come within the scope of our consciousness in understanding, feeling, and will. But we must not suppose that the measure of our understanding or experience is the measure of the Spirit's working. In every distinct and particular movement of the believer in the way of holiness there is an energizing activity of the Holy Spirit, and when we try to discover what the mode of that exercise of his grace and power is we realize

how far we are from being able to diagnose the secret workings of the Spirit.

(2) It is imperative that we realize our complete dependence upon the Holy Spirit. We must not forget, of course, that our activity is enlisted to the fullest extent in the process of sanctification. But we must not rely upon our own strength of resolution or purpose. It is when we are weak that we are strong. It is by grace that we are being saved as surely as by grace we have been saved. If we are not keenly sensitive to our own helplessness, then we can make the use of the means of sanctification the minister of self-righteousness and pride and thus defeat the end of sanctification. We must rely not upon the means of sanctification but upon the God of all grace. Self-confident moralism promotes pride, and sanctification promotes humility and contrition.

(3) It is as the Spirit of Christ and as the Spirit of him who raised up Christ from the dead that the Holy Spirit sanctifies. We may not think of the Spirit as operative in us apart from the risen and glorified Christ. The sanctifying process is not only dependent upon the death and resurrection of Christ in its initiation; it is also dependent upon the death and resurrection of Christ in its continuance. It is by the efficacy and virtue which proceed from the exalted Lord that sanctification is carried on, and such virtue belongs to the exalted Lord by reason of his death and resurrection. It is by the Spirit that this virtue is communicated. Perhaps the most significant passage in this connection is 2 Corinthians 3:17-18, where Paul says that the Lord is the Spirit and then indicates that the transforming process by which we are transformed into the Lord's image is by "the Spirit of the Lord" or, perhaps more accurately, "the Lord of the Spirit." However we may interpret the expression at the end of verse 18, it is apparent that the sanctifying work of the Spirit not only consists in progressive conformation to the image of Christ, but is also

dependent upon the activity of the exalted Lord (*cf.* 1 Cor. 15:45). It is the peculiar prerogative and function of the Holy Spirit to glorify Christ by taking of the things of Christ and showing them unto the people of God (*cf.* John 16:14, 16; 2 Cor. 3:17-18). It is as the indwelling Spirit that he does this and as the advocate with believers (John 14:16-17).

The Means of Sanctification

While we are constantly dependent upon the supernatural agency of the Holy Spirit, we must also take account of the fact that sanctification is a process that draws within its scope the conscious life of the believer. The sanctified are not passive or quiescent in this process. Nothing shows this more clearly than the exhortation of the apostle: "Work out your own salvation with fear and trembling; for it is God who works in you both to will and to do for his good pleasure" (Phil. 2:12-13). The salvation referred to here is not the salvation already in possession but the eschatological salvation (*cf.* 1 Thess. 5:8 9; 1 Pet. 1:5, 9; 2:2). And no text sets forth more succinctly and clearly the relation of God's working to our working. God's working in us is not suspended because we work, nor our working suspended because God works. Neither is the relation strictly one of co-operation as if God did his part and we did ours so that the conjunction or co-ordination of both produced the required result. God works in us and we also work. But the relation is that *because* God works we work. All working out of salvation on our part is the effect of God's working in us, not the willing to the exclusion of the doing and not the doing to the exclusion of the willing, but both the willing and the doing. And this working of God is directed to the end of enabling us to will and to do that which is well pleasing to him. We have here not only the explanation of all acceptable activity on our part but we have also the incentive to our willing and working. What the apostle is urging is the necessity of working out our own salvation, and the encouragement he supplies is the assurance that it is God himself who works in us. The more persistently active we are in working, the more persuaded we may be that all the energizing grace and power is of God.

The exhortations to action with which the Scripture is pervaded are all to the effect of reminding us that our whole being is intensely active in that process which has as its goal the predestinating purpose of God that we should be conformed to the image of his Son (Rom. 8:29). Paul says again to the Philippians, "And this I pray that your love may abound yet more and more in knowledge and in all discernment, so that ye may approve the things that are excellent, that ye may be sincere and without offence unto the day of Christ, being filled with the fruit of righteousness which is through Jesus Christ, unto the glory and praise of God" (Phil. 1:9-11). And Peter, in like manner, "Yea, and for this very cause adding on your part all diligence, in your faith supply virtue; and in your virtue knowledge; and in your knowledge self-control; and in your self-control patience; and in your patience godliness; and in your godliness brotherly kindness; and in your brotherly kindness love. For if these things are yours and abound, they make you to be not idle nor unfruitful unto the knowledge of our Lord Jesus Christ" (2 Pet. 1:5-8). It is unnecessary to multiply quotations. The New Testament is strewn with this emphasis (cf. Rom. 12:1-3, 9-21; 13:7-14; 2 Cor. 7:1; Gal. 5:13-16, 25-26; Eph. 4:17-32; Phil. 3:10-17; 4:4-9; Col. 3:1-25; 1 Thess. 5:8-22; Heb. 12:14-16; 13:1-9; James 1:19-27; 2:14-26; 3:13-18; 1 Pet. 1:13-25; 2:11-13, 17; 2 Pet. 3:14-18; 1 John 2:3-11; 3:17-24). Sanctification involves the concentration of thought, of interest, of heart, mind, will, and purpose upon the prize of the high calling of God in Christ Jesus and the engagement of our whole being with those means which God has instituted for the attainment of that destination. Sanctification is the sanctification of persons, and persons are not machines; it is the sanctification of persons renewed after the image of God in knowledge, righteousness, and holiness. The prospect it offers is to know even as we are known and to be holy as God is holy. Every one who has this hope in God purifies himself even as he is pure (I John 3:3).

CHAPTER VIII

Perseverance

E xperience, observation, biblical history, and certain Scripture passages would appear to provide very strong arguments against the doctrine which has been called "The Perseverance of the Saints." Is not the biblical record as well as the history of the church strewn with examples of those who have made shipwreck of the faith? And do we not read that it is "impossible for those who were once enlightened, and have tasted of the heavenly gift, and were made partakers of the Holy Ghost, and have tasted the good word of God, and the powers of the world to come, if they fall away, to renew them again unto repentance" (Heb. 6:4-6)? Did not our Lord himself say, "I am the true vine, and my Father is the husbandman. Every branch in me that beareth not fruit he taketh away.... If a man abide not in me, he is cast forth as a branch and is withered" (John 15:1-2, 6)? Yes, faced with the facts of history and with Scripture passages like those quoted it must be said that the interpretation of Scripture on this question is not a task for the indolent. What does apostasy mean? What does the Scripture mean by falling away?

In order to place the doctrine of perseverance in proper light we need to know what it is not. It does not mean that every one who professes faith in Christ and who is accepted as a believer in the fellowship of the saints is secure for eternity and may entertain the assurance of eternal salvation. Our Lord himself warned his followers in the days of his flesh when he said to those Jews who believed on him, "If ye continue in my word, then are ye truly my disciples, and ye shall know the truth, and the truth shall make you free" (John 8:31-32). He set up a criterion by which true disciples might be distinguished, and that criterion is continuance in Jesus' word. It is just what we find elsewhere when Jesus said, "He that endureth to the end, the same shall be saved" (Matt. 10:22). It is the criterion applied also in the epistle to the Hebrews when the writer says, "We are partakers of Christ, if we hold fast the beginning of our confidence stedfast unto the end" (Heb. 4:14). It is the same lesson that is the burden of Jesus' teaching in John 15 in connection with the parable of the vine and the branches. "If a man abide not in me, he is cast forth as a branch and is withered" (John 15:6). The crucial test of true faith is endurance to the end, abiding in Christ, and continuance in his word.

This emphasis of Scripture should teach us two things. (1) It provides us with the meaning of falling away, of apostasy. It is possible to give all the outward signs of faith in Christ and obedience to him, to witness for a time a good confession and show great zeal for Christ and his kingdom and then lose all interest and become indifferent, if not hostile, to the claims of Christ and of his kingdom. It is the lesson of seed sown on rocky ground — the seed took root, it sprang up, but when the sun arose it was scorched and brought forth no fruit to perfection (cf. Mark 4:5-6, 16-17). There is, of course, a great deal of variation within this class of people. Some appear to be converted, they boil over with enthusiasm for a little while, and then suddenly cool off. They disappear from the fellowship of the saints. Others do not show the same enthusiasm; their attachment to the faith of Christ has never been one of very pronounced character. But in the course of time it becomes precariously tenuous and finally the tie is completely broken — they walk no more in the path of the righteous. (2) We must appreciate the lengths and the heights to which a temporary faith may carry those who have it. This is brought to our attention to a certain extent in the parable of the sower. Those compared to seed sown on rocky soil received the word with joy and continued in this joyful experience for a season. In terms of the similitude there was the blade and sometimes there may be the ear. There is not only germination; there is also growth. The only defect is that there is never the full com in the ear. To a greater extent it is brought to our attention in the language of the epistle to the Hebrews when it speaks of those "who were once enlightened and tasted of the heavenly gift and were made partakers of the Holy Spirit and tasted the good word of God and the powers of the age to come" (Heb. 6:5-6). It staggers us to think of the terms of this description as applicable to those who may fall away. They advise us, however, of forces that are operative in the kingdom of God and of the influence these forces may exert upon those who finally demonstrate that they had not been radically and savingly affected by them. It is this same fact of apostasy from faith and its corresponding experiences that Peter deals with in 2 Peter 2:20-22. It cannot be doubted but Peter has in view persons who had the knowledge of the Lord and Savior Jesus Christ, who had known the way of righteousness, and who had thereby escaped the pollutions of the world but who had again become entangled in these pollutions and had turned from the holy commandment delivered unto them so that "it is happened unto them according to the true proverb, The dog is turned to his own vomit again; and the sow that was washed to her wallowing in the mire." The Scripture itself, therefore, leads us to the conclusion that it is possible to have very uplifting, ennobling, reforming, and exhilarating experience of the power and truth of the gospel, to come into such close contact with the supernatural forces which are operative in God's kingdom of grace that these forces produce effects in us which to human observation are hardly distinguishable from those produced by God's regenerating and sanctifying grace and yet be not partakers of Christ and heirs of eternal life. A doctrine of perseverance that fails to take account of such a possibility and of its actuality in certain cases is a distorted one and ministers to a laxity which is quite contrary to the interests of perseverance. Indeed it is not the doctrine of perseverance at all.

This leads us to a better understanding of the aptness and expressiveness of the designation, "The Perseverance of the Saints." It is not in the best interests of the doctrine involved to substitute the designation, "The Security of the Believer," not because the latter is wrong in itself but because the other formula is much more carefully and inclusively framed. The very expression, "The Perseverance of the Saints" in itself guards against every notion or suggestion to the effect that a believer is secure, that is to say, secure as to his eternal salvation, quite irrespective of the extent to which he may fall into sin and backslide from faith and holiness. It guards against any such way of construing the status of the believer because that way of stating the doctrine is pernicious and perverse. It is not true that the believer is secure however much he may fall into sin and unfaithfulness. Why is this not true? It is not true because it sets up an impossible combination. It is true that a believer sins; he may fall into grievous sin and backslide for lengthy periods. But it is also true that a believer cannot abandon himself to sin; he cannot come under the dominion of sin; he cannot be guilty of certain kinds of unfaithfulness. And therefore it is utterly wrong to say that a believer is secure quite irrespective of his subsequent life of sin and unfaithfulness. The truth is that the faith of Jesus Christ is *always respective* of the life of holiness and fidelity. And so it is never proper to think of a believer irrespective of the fruits in faith and holiness. To say that a believer is secure whatever may be the extent of his addiction to sin in his subsequent life is to abstract faith in Christ from its very definition and it ministers to that abuse which turns the grace of God into lasciviousness. The doctrine of perseverance is the doctrine that believers *persevere;* it cannot be too strongly stressed that it is the *perseverance* of the saints. And that means that the saints, those united to Christ by the effectual call of the Father and indwelt by the Holy Spirit, will persevere unto the end. If they persevere, they endure, they continue. It is not at all that they will be saved irrespective of their perseverance or their continuance, but that they will assuredly persevere. Consequently the security that is theirs is inseparable from their perseverance. Is this not what Jesus said? "He that endureth to the end, the same shall be saved."

It is to the same effect that Peter writes of those who have the living hope of "an inheritance incorruptible, and undefiled, and that fadeth not away, reserved in heaven." They are those who "are kept by the power of God through faith unto salvation ready to be revealed in the last time" (1 Pet. 1:4-5). There are three things particularly noteworthy: (1) they are kept; (2) they are kept through faith; (3) they are kept unto the final consummation, the salvation to be revealed in the last time. It is not keeping for a little while, but to the end, and it is not keeping irrespective of faith but through faith. Let us not then take refuge in our sloth or encouragement in our lust from the abused doctrine of the security of the believer. But let us appreciate the doctrine of the perseverance of the saints and recognize that we may entertain the faith of our security in Christ only as we persevere in faith and holiness to the end. It was nothing less than the goal of the resurrection to life and glory that Paul had in mind when he wrote,

"Brethren, I count not myself to have apprehended: but this one thing I do, forgetting those things which are behind, and reaching forth unto those things which are before, I press towards the mark for the prize of the high calling of God in Christ Jesus" (Phil. 3:13-14).

The perseverance of the saints reminds us very forcefully that only those who persevere to the end are truly saints. We do not attain to the prize of the high calling of God in Christ Jesus automatically. Perseverance means the engagement of our persons in the most intense and concentrated devotion to those means which God has ordained for the achievement of his saving purpose. The scriptural doctrine of perseverance has no affinity with the quietism and antinomianism which are so prevalent in evangelical circles.

But while it is true that only those who persevere are saints, the question remains: will the saints persevere? Is it so ordained and provided by God that those who do truly believe in Christ will persevere to the end? The answer to this question is, emphatically, yes. Here it is just as important to deny the Arminian tenet that the saints may "fall from grace" as it is to counteract antinomian presumption and licence.

It is true, of course, that the expression "fallen from grace" appears in the Scripture (Gal. 5:4). But Paul is here dealing not with the question as to whether or not a believer may fall out of the favor of God and finally perish but with defection from the pure doctrine of justification by grace as opposed to justification by works of law. What Paul is saying in effect is that if we seek to be justified by the works of the law in any way or degree whatsoever then we have abandoned or fallen away entirely from justification by grace. We cannot have a mixture of grace and works in justification; it is one or the other. If we interject works to any degree then we have given up grace and we are debtors to do the whole law (cf. Gal. 5:3). This teaching of Paul is germane to the whole question of perseverance. For no one tenet of our faith is more important in the promotion of perseverance than the doctrine of justification by grace alone through faith alone. But Paul is not dealing here with believers who fall out of the grace of God. That would be inconsistent with Paul's own clear teaching elsewhere in his epistles. Indeed, it is to Paul's own teaching that we may appeal first of all to establish the position that the saints will persevere.

Who are the "saints" in terms of the New Testament? They are those who are called to be saints, the called of Jesus Christ (Rom. 1:6-7). It is quite impossible to separate what the New Testament means by sainthood from the effectual call by which sinners are ushered into the fellowship of Jesus Christ (1 Cor. 1:9). Now we must ask: what in Paul's teaching are the relations of this calling which constitutes a person a saint? He tells us in Romans 8:28-30. Here we have an unbreakable chain of events proceeding from God's eternal purpose in foreknowledge and predestination to the glorification of the people of God. It is impossible to remove calling from this setting. The called are called according to purpose (ver. 28); the purpose is antecedent to the calling. And that is what Paul says again in verses 29 and 30 where he expounds the purpose of God in terms of foreknowledge and predestination — "whom he did foreknow, he also did predestinate . . . and whom he did predestinate, them he also called." Moreover, just as calling has its antecedents in foreknowledge and predestination, so it has its consequents in justification and glorification — "whom he called, them he also justified, and whom he justified, them he also glorified" (ver. 30). In connection with the subject in hand, we cannot evade the significance of this passage. Those with whom we are now concerned are saints, the called of Jesus Christ; they are those who are justified by the faith of Jesus Christ. A true Christian cannot be defined in lower terms than one who has been called and justified. And therefore the question is: may one who has been called and justified fall away and come short of eternal salvation? Paul's answer is inescapable — the called and the justified will be glorified. Likewise, if we proceed in the other direction, we reach the same result. The called are those who have been predestinated to be conformed to the image of God's Son (ver. 29). Is it possible to conceive of God's predestinating purpose as being defeated? Not even an Arminian will say that. For he believes that God predestinates to eternal salvation those whom he foresees will persevere to the end and be saved.

We need to appreciate what is at stake in this controversy. If saints may fall away and be finally lost, then the called and the justified may fall away and be lost. But that is what the inspired apostle says will not happen and cannot happen — whom God calls and justifies he also glorifies. And that glorification is nothing less than conformity to the image of God's own Son. It is that of which Paul speaks when he says that God "will transfigure the body of our humiliation that it may be conformed to the body of his (Christ's) glory" (Phil. 3:21) and which in Romans 8:23 he calls "the adoption, the redemption of our body." The denial of the perseverance of the saints devastates the explicit import of the apostle's teaching.

We could rest the argument for the doctrine of perseverance on this one passage. But the Scripture provides us with added confirmation. It is well to remember the words of him who spoke as never man spoke; who came down from heaven to do the will of him that sent him that of all whom the Father had given him he should lose nothing but should raise it up at the last day (John 6:39). Surely no one will deny that a saint in New Testament terms is one who believes on Christ. A saint is a believer. And what does Jesus say respecting a believer? "For this is the will of my Father, that every one who sees the

Son and believes on him may have eternal life, and I will raise him up at the last day" (John 6:40). Are we to entertain even the remotest suspicion that this will of the Father will be defeated? Jesus here assures us that it will not. For he defines for us the sequel. He says not only that it is the will of the Father that every one who believes on him may have eternal life but also that "he will raise him in the last day." Lest we should be in doubt as to the character of this resurrection in the last day he informs us in the preceding verse that the resurrection in the last day is in contrast with the losing of anything given him by the Father. In other words, the resurrection in the last day of which Jesus is here speaking is the resurrection that is conjoined with the securing from loss of that which the Father had given to him — "and this is the will of him who sent me, that everything which he hath given to me I should not lose anything of it, but I will raise it up at the last day" (ver. 39). And does not Jesus give us the most pointed assurance that a believer cannot perish when he says, "him that cometh unto me I will in no wise cast out" (ver. 37)? To come unto him is simply to believe on him. And the security that Jesus en visions and guarantees stops not one whit short of the resurrection to life at the last day.

But this is not all. We do well to examine these discourses of Jesus as recorded in the gospel of John still further. Jesus also says "Every one whom the Father giveth to me shall come to me" (6:37). Wherever there is the giving on the part of the Father there is the inevitable consequent or concomitant of coming to Christ, that is to say, of believing on him. But it is also true that wherever there is coming to Christ there is also the giving on the part of the Father, for Jesus also says that no one can come unto him except the Father draw him (6:44) and except it were given him of the Father (6:65). In this discourse we shall have to regard the giving of men to Christ and the drawing of men to Christ on the part of the Father as two aspects of the same event, two ways in which the same event may be viewed. The drawing of the Father views the event as action exerted upon men, the giving to Christ as donation on the part of the Father to the Son. It is impossible to think of them as separable. The sum of the matter then is that no one can come to Christ except by donation to Christ on the Father's part. And we have found already in Jesus' express words that every one thus donated comes to Christ and believes on him. Hence giving by the Father and coming to Christ on the part of men are inseparable — either cannot exist without the other and wherever the one is the other is.

If we turn now to John 10 we shall find, on this background, conclusive confirmation of the truth that believers cannot perish. Jesus again is talking of those who have been given him by the Father. We cannot dissociate the giving spoken of here from the giving spoken of in John 6, even though Jesus introduces a new designation by which to characterize the persons concerned, namely, that they are his sheep. What is it that Jesus says? "My Father who hath given them to me is greater than all, and no one is able to snatch out of the Father's hand. I and the Father are one" (10:29-30). When we inquire as to the force of this that no one is able to snatch out of the Father's hand, we find it in the preceding words of Jesus: "I give unto them eternal life, and they shall never perish, and no one will snatch them out of my hand" (10:28). What Jesus is dealing with is obviously the infallible security of those who have been given unto him by the Father — "they shall never perish." And that same security is guaranteed by the fact that no one will snatch them out of his hand. It is to confirm that truth that he says, "My Father who gave them to me is greater than all, and no one can snatch out of the Father's hand." The guarantee of infallible preservation is that the persons given to the Son are in the Son's hand and though given to the Son they are still mysteriously in the Father's hand. From the hand of neither can any one snatch them. This is the heritage of those who are given by the Father.

But we must also remember that all who are given to Christ come to Christ, that is, believe on him, and all who believe on him are those who have been given to him. Therefore it is not simply of those who have been given to him by the Father that Jesus is speaking in John 10:28, 29; he is speaking also of believers. We have found from the passages in John 6 that those given are believers and believers are those given. Hence, of all believers, that is, of all who come to Christ in terms of John 6:37, 44, 45, 65, it can be said on the authority of him who is the truth, the true God and eternal life, that believers in Jesus' name will never perish — they will be raised up in the last day to the resurrection of the blessed. In Paul's language, they will "attain unto the resurrection of the dead" (Phil. 3:11).

Have we not in this truth new reason to marvel at the grace of God and the immutability of his love. It is the indissolubility of the bond of the covenant of God's grace that undergirds this precious article of faith. "For the mountains shall depart, and the hills be removed; but my lovingkindness shall not depart from thee, neither shall my covenant of peace be removed, saith the Lord that hath mercy on thee" (Isa. 54:10).

CHAPTER IX

Union with Christ

In these studies we are dealing with the application of redemption. Intelligent readers may have wondered why there has not been up to this point some treatment of union with Christ. Obviously it is an important aspect of the application of redemption and, if we did not take account of it, not only would our presentation of the application of redemption be defective but our view of the Christian life would be gravely distorted. Nothing is more central or basic than union and communion with Christ.

There is, however, a good reason why the subject of union with Christ should not be co-ordinated with the other phases of the application of redemption with which we have dealt. That reason is that union with Christ is in itself a very broad and embracive subject. It is not simply a step in the application of redemption; when viewed, according to the teaching of Scripture, in its broader aspects it underlies every step of the application of redemption. Union with Christ is really the central truth of the whole doctrine of salvation not only in its application but also in its once-for-all accomplishment in the finished work of Christ. Indeed the whole process of salvation has its origin in one phase of union with Christ and salvation has in view the realization of other phases of union with Christ. This can be readily seen if we remember that brief expression which is so common in the New Testament, namely, "in Christ." It is that which is meant by "in Christ" that we have in mind when we speak of "union with Christ." It is quite apparent that the Scripture applies the expression "in Christ" to much more than the application of redemption. A certain aspect of union with Christ, it is true, belongs strictly to the application of redemption. With that we shall deal later. But we would not deal properly with the subject of union with Christ unless we set forth, first of all, its broader meaning. We would not be able to appreciate that which falls within the application of redemption if we did not relate it to that which is broader.

The breadth of union with Christ can be seen if we survey the teaching of Scripture respecting it. When we do this we see how far back it goes and how far forward.

The fountain of salvation itself in the eternal election of the Father is "in Christ." Paul says: "Blessed be the God and Father of our Lord Jesus Christ, who hath blessed us with all spiritual blessings in the heavenlies in Christ, even as he chose us in him before the foundation of the world" (Eph. 1:3-4). The Father elected from eternity, but he elected in Christ. We are not able to understand all that is involved, but the fact is plain enough that there was no election of the Father in eternity apart from Christ. And that means that those who will be saved were not even contemplated by the Father in the ultimate counsel of his predestinating love apart from union with Christ — they were *chosen* in Christ. As far back as we can go in tracing salvation to its fountain we find "union with Christ"; it is not something tacked on; it is there from the outset.

It is also because the people of God were in Christ when he gave his life a ransom and redeemed by his blood that salvation has been secured for them; they are represented as united to Christ in his death, resurrection, and exaltation to heaven (Rom. 6:2-11; Eph. 2:4-6; Col. 3:3-4). "In the beloved," Paul says, "we have redemption through his blood" (Eph. 1:7). Hence we may never think of the work of redemption wrought once for all by Christ apart from the union with his people which was effected in the election of the Father before the foundation of the world. In other words, we may never think of redemption in abstraction from the mysterious arrangements of God's love and wisdom and grace by which Christ was united to his people and his people were united to him when he died upon the accursed tree and rose again from the dead. This is but another way of saying that the church is the body of Christ and "Christ loved the church and gave himself for it" (Eph. 5:25).

It is in Christ that the people of God are created anew. "We are his workmanship, created in Christ Jesus unto good works" (Eph. 2:10). Here Paul is insisting upon the great truth that by grace, not works, we are saved. Salvation has its inception in God's grace. And this is certified by the fact that we are saved by a new creation in Christ. It should not surprise us that the beginning of salvation in actual possession should be in union with Christ because we have found already that it is in Christ that salvation had its origin in the eternal election of the Father and that it is in Christ salvation was once for all secured by Jesus' ransom blood. We could not think of such union with Christ as suspended when the people of God become the actual partakers of redemption — they are created anew in Christ.

But not only does the new life have its inception in Christ; it is also continued by virtue of the same relationship to him It is in Christ that Christian life and behavior are conducted (Rom. 6:4; 1 Cor. 1:4-5; *cf.* 1 Cor. 6:15-17). The new life believers live they live in the fellowship of Jesus' resurrection; in everything they are made rich in him in all utterance and in all knowledge.

It is in Christ that believers die. They have fallen asleep in Christ or through Christ and they are dead in Christ (1 Thess. 4:14, 16). Could anything illustrate the indissolubility of union with Christ more plainly than the fact that this union is not severed even in death? Death, of course, is real — spirit and body are rent asunder. But the separated elements of the person are still united to Christ. "Precious in the sight of the Lord is the death of his saints" (Ps. 116:15).

Finally, it is in Christ that the people of God will be resurrected and glorified. It is in Christ they will be made alive when the last trumpet will sound and the dead will be raised incorruptible (1 Cor. 15:22). It is with Christ they will be glorified (Rom. 8:17).

We thus see that union with Christ has its source in the election of God the Father before the foundation of the world and it has its fruition in the glorification of the sons of God. The perspective of God's people is not narrow; it is broad and it is long. It is not confined to space and time; it has the expanse of eternity. Its orbit has two foci, one the electing love of God the Father in the counsels of eternity, the other glorification with Christ in the manifestation of his glory. The former has no beginning, the latter has no end. Glorification with Christ at his coming will be but the beginning of a consummation that will encompass the ages of the ages. "So shall we ever be with the Lord" (1 Thess. 4:17). It is a perspective with a past and with a future, but neither the past nor the future is bounded by what we know as our temporal history. And because temporal history falls within such a perspective it has meaning and hope. What is it that binds past and present and future together in the life of faith and in the hope of glory? Why does the believer entertain the thought of God's determinate counsel with such joy? Why can he have patience in the perplexities and adversities of the present? Why can he have confident assurance with reference to the future and rejoice in hope of the glory of God? It is because he cannot think of past, present, or future apart from union with Christ. It is union with Christ now in the virtue of his death and the power of his resurrection that certifies to him the reality of his election in Christ before the foundation of the world — he is blessed by the Father with all spiritual blessings in the heavenlies in Christ just as he was chosen in Christ from eternal ages (cf. Eph. 1:3-4). And he has the seal of an eternal inheritance because it is in Christ that he is sealed with the Holy Spirit of promise as the earnest of his inheritance unto the redemption of the purchased possession (cf. Eph. 1:13-14). Apart from union with Christ we cannot view past, present, or future with anything but dismay and Christless dread. By union with Christ the whole complexion of time and eternity is changed and the people of God may rejoice with joy unspeakable and full of glory.

Union with Christ is a very inclusive subject. It embraces the wide span of salvation from its ultimate source in the eternal election of God to its final fruition in the glorification of the elect. It is not simply a phase of the application of redemption; it underlies every aspect of redemption both in its accomplishment and in its application. Union with Christ binds all together and insures that to all for whom Christ has purchased redemption he effectually applies and communicates the same.

But union with Christ is an important part of the application of redemption. We do not become *actual* partakers of Christ until redemption is effectually applied. Paul in writing to the believers at Ephesus reminded them that they were chosen in Christ before the foundation of the world, but he also reminded them that there was a time when *they* were "without Christ, alienated from the commonwealth of Israel and strangers from the covenants of promise, having no hope and without God in the world" (Eph. 2:12) and that they were "by nature children of wrath even as others" (Eph. 2:3). Although they had been chosen in Christ before times eternal, yet they were Christless until they were called effectually into the fellowship of God's Son (1 Cor. 1:9). Hence it is by the effectual call of God the Father that men are made partakers of Christ and enter into the enjoyment of the blessings of redemption. Only then do they know the fellowship of Christ.

What is the nature of this union with Christ which is effected by the call of God? There are several things to be said in answer to this question.

1. It is *Spiritual*. Few words in the New Testament have been subjected to more distortion than the word "Spiritual." Frequently it is used to denote what is little more than vague sentimentality. "Spiritual" in the New Testament refers to that which is of the Holy Spirit. The spiritual man is the person who is indwelt and controlled by the Holy Spirit and a spiritual state of mind is a state of mind that is produced and maintained by the Holy Spirit. Hence when we say that union with Christ is *Spiritual* we mean, first of all, that the bond of this union is the Holy Spirit himself. "For in one Spirit were we all baptized into one body, whether Jews or Greeks, whether bond or free. And we were all made to drink of one Spirit" (1 Cor. 12:13; cf. 1 Cor. 6:17, 19; Rom. 8:9-11; 1 John 3:24; 4:13). We need to appreciate far more than we have been wont to the close interdependence of Christ and the Holy Spirit in the operations of saving grace. The Holy Spirit is the Spirit of Christ; the Spirit is the Spirit of the Lord and Christ is the Lord of the Spirit (cf. Rom. 8:9; 2 Cor. 3:18; 1 Pet. 1:11). Christ dwells in us if his Spirit dwells in us, and he dwells in us by the Spirit. Union with Christ is a great mystery. That the Holy Spirit is the bond of this union does not diminish the mystery but this truth does throw a flood of light upon the mystery and it also guards the mystery against sensuous notions, on the one hand, and pure sentimentality, on the other.

This brings us to note, in the second place, that union
with Christ is *Spiritual* because it is a spiritual relationship
that is in view. It is not the kind of union that we have in
the Godhead — three persons in one God. It is not the kind
of union we have in the person of Christ — two natures in
one person. It is not the kind of union we have in man —
body and soul constituting a human being. It is not simply
the union of feeling, affection, understanding, mind, heart,
will, and purpose. Here we have union which we are unable
to define specifically. But it is union of an intensely spiritual
character consonant with the nature and work of the Holy
Spirit so that in a real way surpassing our power of analysis
Christ dwells in his people and his people dwell in him.

2. It is *Mystical*. When we use the word "mystical" in this
connection it is well to take our starting-point from the word
"mystery" as it is used in the Scripture. We are liable to use
the word to designate something that is completely unintelligible and of which we cannot have any understanding. That
is not the sense of Scripture. The apostle in Romans 16:25-26
sets the points for the understanding of this term. There Paul
speaks of "the revelation of the mystery hid from times eternal, but manifested now through the Scriptures of the prophets according to the commandment of the eternal God and
made known unto the obedience of faith among all nations."
There are four things to be observed about this mystery. (1)
It was kept secret from times eternal — it was something
hid in the mind and counsel of God. (2) It did not continue
to be kept hid — it was manifested and made known in accordance with the will and commandment of God. (3) This
revelation on God's part was mediated through and deposited in the Scripture — it was revealed to all nations and is no
longer a secret. (4) This revelation is directed to the end that
all nations may come to the obedience of faith. A mystery is,
therefore, something which eye hath not seen nor ear heard

neither hath entered into the heart of man but which God has revealed unto us by his Spirit and which by revelation and faith comes to be known and appropriated by men.

That union with Christ is such a mystery is apparent. In speaking of union with Christ and after comparing it with the union that exists between man and wife, Paul says: "This mystery is great, but I speak of Christ and of the church" (Eph. 5:32). And again Paul speaks of "the riches of the glory of this mystery among the Gentiles, which is Christ in you, the hope of glory" and describes it as "the mystery which has been hid from the ages and from the generations, but now has been manifested to his saints" (Col. 1:26-27). Union with Christ is mystical because it is a mystery. That fact that it is a mystery underlines the preciousness of it and the intimacy of the relation it entails.

The wide range of similitude used in Scripture to illustrate union with Christ is very striking. On the highest level of being it is compared to the union which exists between the persons of the trinity in the Godhead. This is staggering, but it is the case (John 14:23; 17:21-23). On the lowest level it is compared to the relation that exists between the stones of a building and the chief corner stone (Eph. 2:19-22; 1 Pet. 2:4-5). In between these two limits there is a variety of similitude drawn from different levels of being and relationship. It is compared to the union that existed between Adam and all of posterity (Rom. 5:12-19; 1 Cor. 15:19-49). It is compared to the union that exists between man and wife (Eph. 5:22-33; cf. John 3:29). It is compared to the union that exists between the head and the other members in the human body (Eph. 4:15-16). It is compared to the relation of the vine to the branches (John 15). Hence we have analogy drawn from the various strata of being, ascending from the inanimate realm to the very life of the persons of the Godhead.

This should teach us a great principle. It is obvious that

we must not reduce the nature and the mode of union with Christ to the measure of the kind of union that exists between the chief corner stone and the other stones in the building, nor to the measure of the kind of union that exists between the vine and the branches, nor to that of the head and the other members of the body, nor even to that of husband and wife. The mode, nature, and kind of union differ in the different cases. There is similitude but not identity. But just as we may not reduce the union between Christ and his people to the level of the union that exists on these other strata of being, so we must not raise it to the level of the union that exists within the Godhead. Similitude here again does not mean identity. Union with Christ does not mean that we are incorporated into the life of the Godhead. That is one of the distortions to which this great truth has been subjected. But the process of thought by which such a view has been adopted neglects one of the simplest principles which must always guide our thinking, namely, that analogy does not mean identity. When we make a comparison we do not make an equation. Of all the kinds of union or unity that exist for creatures the union of believers with Christ is the highest. The greatest mystery of being is the mystery of the trinity — three persons in one God. The great mystery of godliness is the mystery of the incarnation, that the Son of God became man and was manifest in the flesh (1 Tim. 3:16). But the greatest mystery of creaturely relations is the union of the people of God with Christ. And the mystery of it is attested by nothing more than this that it is compared to the union that exists between the Father and the Son in the unity of the Godhead.

It has been customary to use the word mystical to express the mysticism which enters into the exercise of faith. It is necessary for us to recognize that there is an intelligent mysticism in the life of faith. Believers are called into the fellowship of Christ and fellowship means communion. The life of faith is one of living union and communion with the exalted and ever-present Redeemer. Faith is directed not only to a Redeemer who has come and completed once for all a work of redemption. It is directed to him not merely as the one who died but as the one who rose again and who ever lives as our great high priest and advocate. And because faith is directed to him as living Savior and Lord, fellowship reaches the zenith of its exercise. There is no communion among men that is comparable to fellowship with Christ — he communes with his people and his people commune with him in conscious reciprocal love. "Whom having not seen ye love," wrote the apostle Peter, "in whom though now ye see him not yet believing ye rejoice with joy unspeakable and full of glory" (1 Pet. 1:8). The life of faith is the life of love, and the life of love is the life of fellowship, or mystic communion with him who ever lives to make intercession for his people and who can be touched with the feeling of our infirmities. It is fellowship with him who has an inexhaustible reservoir of sympathy with his people's temptations, afflictions, and infirmities because he was tempted in all points like as they are, yet without sin. The life of true faith cannot be that of cold metallic assent. It must have the passion and warmth of love and communion because communion with God is the crown and apex of true religion. "Truly our fellowship is with the Father and with his Son Jesus Christ" (1 John 1:3).

Union with Christ is the central truth of the whole doctrine of salvation. All to which the people of God have been predestined in the eternal election of God, all that has been secured and procured for them in the once-for-all accomplishment of redemption, all of which they become the actual partakers in the application of redemption, and all that by God's grace they will become in the state of consummated bliss is embraced within the compass of union and communion with Christ. As we found earlier in these studies, it is adoption into the family of God as sons and daughters of the Lord God Almighty that accords to the people of God the apex of blessing and privilege. But we cannot think of adoption apart from union with Christ. It is significant that the election in Christ before the foundation of the world is election unto the adoption of sons. When Paul says that the Father chose a people in Christ before the foundation of the world that they should be holy he also adds that in love he predestinated them unto adoption through Jesus Christ (Eph. 1:4-5). Apparently election to holiness is parallel to pre-destination to adoption — these are two ways of expressing the same great truth. They disclose to us the different facets which belong to the Father's election. Hence union with Christ and adoption are complementary aspects of this amazing grace. Union with Christ reaches its zenith in adoption and adoption has its orbit in union with Christ. The people of God are "heirs of God and joint-heirs with Christ" (Rom. 8:17). All things are theirs whether life or death or things present or things to come, all are theirs, because they are Christ's and Christ is God's (1 Cor. 3:22-23). They are united to him in whom are hid all the treasures of wisdom and knowledge and they are complete in him who is the head of all principality and power.

It is out of the measureless fullness of grace and truth, of wisdom and power, of goodness and love, of righteousness and faithfulness which resides in him that God's people draw for all their needs in this life and for the hope of the life to come. There is no truth, therefore, more suited to impart confidence and strength, comfort and joy in the Lord than this one of union with Christ. It also promotes sanctification, not only because all sanctifying grace is derived from Christ as the crucified and exalted Redeemer, but also because the recognition of fellowship with Christ and of the high privilege it entails incites to gratitude, obedience, and devotion.

Union means also communion and communion constrains a humble, reverent, loving walk with him who died and rose again that he might be our Lord. "But whoso keeps his word in him verily is the love of God perfected. By this we know that we are in him. He that says he abides in him ought himself also so to walk even as he walked" (1 John 2:5-6). "Abide in me, and I in you. As the branch cannot bear fruit of itself except it abide in the vine, no more can ye except ye abide in me" (John 15:4).

There is another phase of the subject of union with Christ that must not be omitted. If it were overlooked there would be a serious defect in our understanding and appreciation of the implications of this union. These are the implications which arise from the relations of Christ to the other persons of the trinity and from our relations to the other persons of the trinity by reason of our union with Christ. Jesus himself said, "I and the Father are one" (John 10:30). We should expect, therefore, that union with Christ would bring us into similar relation with the Father. This is exactly what our Lord himself tells us. "If a man love me, he will keep my word, and my Father will love him, and we will come unto him and make our abode with him" (John 14:23). The thought is overwhelming but it is unmistakable — the Father as well as Christ comes and makes his abode with the believer. Perhaps even more striking is another word of Jesus. "Not for these only do I ask, but also for those who believe on me through their word, in order that they all may be one, as thou, Father, art in me and I in thee, in order that they also may be in us, that the world may believe that thou hast sent me. And I have given to them the glory which thou hast given me, in order that they may be one as we are one. I in them and thou in me, in order that they may be perfected in one, that the world may know that thou hast sent me and hast loved them as thou hast loved me" (John 17:20-23). And not only is it the

Father who is united with believers and dwells in them. Jesus tells us likewise of the indwelling of the Holy Spirit. "And I will pray the Father and he will give you another Comforter that he may be with you for ever, the Spirit of truth, whom the world cannot receive, because it sees him not neither knows him. But ye know him, because he dwells with you and shall be in you" (John 14:16-17). It is union, therefore, with the Father and with the Son and with the Holy Spirit that union with Christ draws along with it. It is this testimony of Jesus himself that the apostles reiterate when John says, "And truly our fellowship is with the Father and with his Son Jesus Christ" (1 John 1:3) and Paul, "If any man does not have the Spirit of Christ, he is none of his" (Rom. 8:9). It is too confined and therefore a distorted conception of union with Christ that we entertain if it is Christ alone that we think of as sustaining such intimacy of relation to the people of God.

Here indeed is mysticism on the highest plane. It is not the mysticism of vague unintelligible feeling or rapture. It is the mysticism of communion with the one true and living God, and it is communion with the one true and living God because and only because it is communion with the three distinct persons of the Godhead in the strict particularity which belongs to each person in that grand economy of saving relationship to us. Believers know the Father and have fellowship with him in his own distinguishing character and operation as the Father. They know the Son and have fellowship with him in his own distinguishing character and operation as the Son, the Savior, the Redeemer, the exalted Lord. They know and have fellowship with the Holy Spirit in his own distinguishing character and operation as the Spirit, the Advocate, the Comforter, the Sanctifier. It is not the blurred confusion of rapturous ecstasy. It is faith solidly founded on the revelation deposited for us in the Scripture and it is faith actively receiving that revelation by the inward witness of the Holy

Spirit. But it is also faith that stirs the deepest springs of emotion in the raptures of holy love and joy. Believers enter into the holy of holies of communion with the triune God and they do so because they have been raised up together and made to sit together in the heavenlies in Christ Jesus (Eph. 2:6). Their life is hid with Christ in God (Col. 3:3). They draw nigh in full assurance of faith having their hearts sprinkled from an evil conscience and their bodies washed with pure water because Christ is not entered into holy places made with hands but into heaven itself now to appear in the presence of God for them (Heb. 9:24).

CHAPTER X

Glorification

G lorification is the final phase of the application of re-demption. It is that which brings to completion the process which begins in effectual calling. Indeed it is the completion of the whole process of redemption. For glorification means the attainment of the goal to which the elect of God were predestinated in the eternal purpose of the Father and it involves the consummation of the redemption secured and procured by the vicarious work of Christ. But when does glorification take place?

It is here that we need to appreciate what glorification really is and how it is to be realized. Glorification does not refer to the blessedness upon which the spirits of believers enter at death. It is true that then the saints, as respects their disembodied spirits, are made perfect in holiness and pass immediately into the presence of the Lord Christ. To be absent from the body is to be present with the Lord (cf. 2 Cor. 5:8). Presence with Christ in his state of glory cannot consist with any of the defilements of sin — the spirits of departed saints are "the spirits of just men made perfect" (Heb. 12:23). The Shorter Catechism sums up the truth when it says: "The souls of believers are at their death made perfect in holiness, and do immediately pass into glory: and their bodies, being still united to Christ, do rest in their graves till the resurrection." Yet, however glorious is the transformation of the people of God at death and however much they may be disposed to say with the apostle that to depart and to be with Christ is far better (*cf.* Phil. 1:23), this is not their glorification. It is not the goal of the believer's hope and expectation. The redemption which Christ has secured for his people is redemption not only from sin but also from all its consequences. Death is the wages of sin and the death of believers does not deliver them from death. The last enemy, death, has not yet been destroyed; it has not yet been swallowed up in victory. Hence glorification has in view the destruction of death itself. It is to dishonor Christ and to undermine the nature of the Christian hope to substitute the blessedness upon which believers enter at death for the glory that is to be revealed when "this corruptible will put on incorruption and this mortal will put on immortality" (1 Cor. 15:54). Preoccupation with the event of death indicates a deflection of faith, of love, and of hope. We who have the firstfruits of the Spirit "groan within ourselves," the apostle reminds us, "waiting for the adoption, the redemption of our body" (Rom. 8:23). That is the glorification. It is the complete and final redemption of the whole person when in the integrity of body and spirit the people of God will be conformed to the image of the risen, exalted, and glorified Redeemer, when the very body of their humiliation will be conformed to the body of Christ's glory (*cf.* Phil 3:21). God is not the God of the dead but of the living and therefore nothing short of resurrection to the full enjoyment of God can constitute the glory to which the living God will lead his redeemed. Christ is the firstbegotten from the dead, the firstfruits of them that have fallen asleep; he is the firstborn among many brethren.

This truth that glorification must wait for the resurrection of the body advises us that glorification is something upon which all the people of God will enter *together* at the same identical point in time. There is no priority for one above another. In this respect it radically differs from death and the glory with Christ upon which saints enter on that event. Each saint of God who dies has his own appointed season and therefore his own time to depart and be with Christ. We can see that this event is highly individualized. But it is not so with glorification. One will not have any advantage over another — all together will be glorified with Christ.

The New Testament lays peculiar stress upon this fact. We might think it unnecessary to accent it. We might say: the important truth is that all will be glorified and all else is of little significance. It is not so. The apostle Paul found it necessary to inform, or perhaps remind, the Thessalonian believers that even those who will not die but be living at the advent of the Lord will not have any advantage over those who died, "because," he says, "the Lord himself will descend from heaven with a shout, with the voice of the archangel and with the trumpet of God, and the dead in Christ will rise first." And so the living and the resurrected dead, who died in Christ, will *together* be snatched up to meet the Lord in the air (1 Thess. 4:16-17). Again, the same apostle says: "Behold, I tell you a mystery: we shall not all sleep, but we shall all be changed, in a moment, in the twinkling of an eye, at the last trumpet: for the trumpet will sound, and the dead will be raised incorruptible, and we shall be changed" (1 Cor. 15:51-52). Glorification, then, is the instantaneous change that will take place for the whole company of the redeemed when Christ will come again the second time without sin unto salvation and will descend from heaven with the shout of triumph over the last enemy. "Then will come to pass the saying that is written, death is swallowed up in victory. O death, where is thy victory? O death, where is thy sting?" (1 Cor. 15:54-55).

There is much for our instruction in this fact that the final act of the application of redemption is one that affects all alike at the same moment of time in the final accomplishment of God's redemptive design. It is as a body that the whole company of the redeemed will be glorified. This is highly consonant with all that of which glorification is the consummation. It is union with Christ that binds together all the phases of redemptive love and grace. It was in Christ the people of God were chosen before the foundation of the world. It was in Christ they were redeemed by his blood — he loved the church and gave himself for it. The people of God were quickened *together* with Christ, and raised up *together* and made to sit *together* in the heavenlies in Christ Jesus (*cf.* Eph. 5:25; 2:5-6). Christ wrought redemption with the design "that he might present the church to himself a glorious church, not having spot or wrinkle or any such thing, but that it should be holy and without blemish" (Eph. 5:27). When heaven's design will reach its grand finale, Christ will come again in the glory of his Father. He will also come in his own glory — it will be "the appearing of the glory of the great God and our Saviour Jesus Christ" (Titus 2:13). But this will also be the revelation of the sons of God (Rom. 8:19). There will be a perfect coincidence of the revelation of the Father's glory, of the revelation of the glory of Christ, and of the liberty of the glory of the children of God. The glorification of the elect will coincide with the final act of the Father in the exaltation and glorification of the Son. "But if children, then heirs; heirs of God, and joint-heirs with Christ; if so be that we suffer with him, that we may be also glorified together" (Rom. 8:17). There is heavenly congruity here, and it is congruity which exemplifies the marvel of divine love, wisdom, and power as it also vindicates the glory of God. "The Lord alone shall be exalted in that day" (Isa.2:11).

Glorification is an event which will affect all the people of God together at the same point of time in the realization of God's redemptive purpose. It will bring to final fruition the purpose and grace which was given in Christ Jesus before times eternal (cf. 2 Tim. 1:9). These truths respecting the glorification of the people of God are complementary to other tenets of the Christian hope.

1. Glorification is associated and bound up with the coming of Christ in glory. The advent of Christ visibly, publicly, and gloriously does not appeal to a great many people who profess the name of Christ. It appears to them to be too naïve for the more advanced and mature perspective of present-day Christians. This attitude is quite akin to that of which Peter warned his readers: "there shall come in the last days scoffers, walking after their own lusts, and saying, Where is the promise of his coming? for since the Fathers fell asleep, all things continue as they were from the beginning of creation" (2 Pet. 3:3-4). It is the same kind of unbelief which entertains doubt respecting the virgin birth of our Lord or denies the substitutionary atonement or spurns the thought of our Lord's bodily and physical resurrection which can be indifferent to the glorious advent of our Lord on the clouds of heaven. And this unbelief becomes peculiarly aggravated when it scorns the very idea of a return of the Lord bodily, visibly, publicly. If that conviction and hope do not stand at the center of our perspective for the future, it is because the barest outlines of our frame of thought are destitute of Christian character. The hope of the believer is centered in the coming of the Savior again the second time without sin unto salvation. Paul calls this "the blessed hope and the appearing of the glory of the great God and our Saviour Christ Jesus" (Titus 2:13). The believer who knows him whom he has believed and loves him whom he has not seen says, "Amen, come Lord Jesus" (Rev. 22:20). So indispensable is the coming of the Lord to the hope of glory that glorification for the believer has no meaning without the manifestation of Christ's glory. Glorification is glorification with Christ. Remove the

latter and we have robbed the glorification of believers of the one thing that enables them to look forward to this event with confidence, with joy unspeakable and full of glory. "But rejoice," Peter wrote, "inasmuch as ye are partakers of Christ's sufferings; that, when his glory shall be revealed, ye may be glad also with exceeding joy" (1 Pet. 4:13).

2. The glorification of believers is associated and bound up with the renewal of creation. It is not only believers who are to be delivered from the bondage of corruption but the creation itself also. "The creation was made subject to vanity, not willingly, but by reason of him who subjected it" (Rom. 8:20). But "the creation itself also will be delivered from the bondage of corruption into the liberty of the glory of the children of God" (Rom. 8:21). And when will this glory of creation be accomplished? Paul leaves us in no doubt. He tells us expressly that the terminus of the groaning and travailing of creation, groaning and travailing because of the bondage of corruption, is nothing other than "the adoption, the redemption of our body" (Rom. 8:23). This is just saying that not only do believers wait for the resurrection as that which will bring the liberty of their glory but the creation itself is also waiting for this same event. And that for which it is waiting is that in which it will share, namely, "the liberty of the glory of the children of God." This is Paul's way of expressing the same truth which is elsewhere described as the new heavens and the new earth. In Peter's words, "We according to his promise look for new heavens and a new earth, wherein dwelleth righteousness" (2 Pet. 3:13). And Peter associates that cosmic regeneration with that which believers look for and hasten, "the coming of the day of God, on account of which the heavens being on fire shall be dissolved and the elements being burned up shall melt" (2 Pet. 3:12).

When we think of glorification, then, it is no narrow perspective that we entertain. It is a renewed cosmos, new heavens and new earth, that we must think of as the context of the believers' glory, a cosmos delivered from all the consequences of sin, in which there will be no more curse but in which righteousness will have complete possession and undisturbed habitation. "And there shall in no wise enter into it anything that defileth, neither whatsoever worketh abomination, or maketh a lie: but they which are written in the Lamb's book of life" (Rev. 21:27). "And there shall be no more curse: but the throne of God and of the Lamb shall be in it; and his servants shall serve him: and they shall see his face; and his name shall be in their foreheads" (Rev. 22:3-4).

One of the heresies which has afflicted the Christian church and has been successful in polluting the stream of Christian thought from the first century of our era to the present is the heresy of regarding matter, that is, material substance, as the source of evil. It has appeared in numerous forms. The apostles had to combat it in their day and the evidence of this appears quite plainly in the New Testament, especially in the epistles. John, for example, had to combat it in the peculiarly aggravated form of denying the reality of Christ's body as one of flesh. And so he had to write: "Many false prophets are gone out into the world. In this ye know the Spirit of God: every spirit that confesseth Jesus Christ as come in the flesh is of God, and every spirit that confesseth not Jesus is not of God" (1 John 4:1-3). The meaning of this is that the confession of Christ Jesus is confession to the effect that he came in flesh and the denial of this is flatly a denial of Jesus. In reference to that heresy the test of orthodoxy was to confess the flesh of Jesus, that is to say that he came with a material, fleshly body.

Another form in which this heresy appeared is to regard salvation as consisting in the emancipation of the soul or spirit of man from the impediments and entanglements of association with the body. Salvation and sanctification progress to the extent to which the immaterial soul overcomes the degrading influences emanating from the material and fleshly. This conception can be made to appear very beautiful and "spiritual," but it is just "beautiful paganism." It is a straight thrust at the biblical doctrine that God created man with body and soul and that he was very good. It is also aimed at the biblical doctrine of sin which teaches that sin has its origin and seat in the spirit of man, not in the material and fleshly.

This heresy has appeared in a very subtle form in connection with the subject of glorification. The direction it has taken in this case is to play on the chord of the immortality of the soul. This seems a very innocent and proper emphasis and, of course, there is some truth in the contention that the soul is immortal. But whenever the focus of interest and emphasis becomes the immortality of the soul, then there is a grave deflection from the biblical doctrine of immortal life and bliss. The biblical doctrine of "immortality." if we may use that term, is the doctrine of *glorification*. And glorification is resurrection. Without resurrection of the body from the grave and the restoration of human nature to its completeness after the pattern of Christ's resurrection on the third day and according to the likeness of the glorified human nature in which he will appear on the clouds of heaven with great power and glory there is no glorification. It is not the vague sentimentality and idealism so characteristic of those whose interest is merely the immortality of the soul. Here we have the concreteness and realism of the Christian hope epitomized in the resurrection to life everlasting and signalized by the descent of Christ from heaven with the voice of the archangel and the trumpet of God.

In like manner the Christian's hope is not indifferent to the material universe around us, the cosmos of God's creation. It was subjected to vanity not willingly; it was cursed for man's sin; it was marred by human apostasy. But it is going to be delivered from the bondage of corruption, and its deliverance will be coincident with the consummation of God's people's redemption. The two are not only coincident as events but they are correlative in hope. Glorification has cosmic proportions. "We according to his promise look for new heavens and a new earth, wherein dwelleth righteousness" (2 Pet. 3:13). "Then the end, when he delivers over the kingdom to God and the Father" and "God will be all in all" (1 Cor. 15:24, 28).

Index of Subjects

abiding in Christ, 160-61, 182
Abraham, reckoned as righteous,
    131
absolute necessity, 6
abstinence from sin, 105-7
Adam, disobedience of, 15
adoption, 83, 89
    distinctiveness of, 139-48
    as judicial act, 140
    and union with Christ, 181
alienation from God, 29-39
"all," in Scripture, 58-59, 70-71
Anselm, 5, 46
antinomianism, 165
apostasy, 160-62
application of redemption, sover-
    eign grace in, 92
Arminians, 165, 167
assent, 116, 117
assurance, 161, 168, 174, 184
atonement, 3
    as efficacious substitution, 74
    efficacy of, 8-9, 10, 55-56, 62-64,
        72-73
    extent of, 57-74
    finality of, 51-53
    historical objectivity of, 50-51
    and justification, 11

meets exigencies of holiness
    and justice, 28
necessity of, 5-10
not eternal, 53
not universal, 60-61, 65-68
uniqueness of, 53-55
Augustine, 5

backsliding, 163
baptism, 101
benefits, of death of Christ to un-
    believers and reprobate, 59-60
Bible
    as norm of interpretation, 75
    universal expressions in, 57-59,
        74
body and soul, 191-92
born of the Spirit, 100, 102-3
Bushnell, Horace, 53-54

calling, 84-85, 87, 91-98
    eternity of, 96
    from the Father, 93-94
    as high, holy, and heavenly, 95
    immutability of, 94-95
    pattern of, 95-97
    priority of, 97
    and regeneration, 88-89
    response to, 99

Index of Scripture References

Index of Scripture References